D1134501

NORWICH CITY
Miscellany

NORWICH CITY
Miscellany

Canaries Trivia,
History, Facts & Stats

EDWARD COUZENS-LAKE

NORWICH CITY
Miscellany

All statistics, facts and figures are correct as of 5th August 2010

© Edward Couzens-Lake

Edward Couzens-Lake has asserted his rights in accordance with the
Copyright, Designs and Patents Act 1988 to be identified as the author of this work.

Published By:
Pitch Publishing (Brighton) Ltd
A2 Yeoman Gate
Yeoman Way
Durrington
BN13 3QZ

Email: info@pitchpublishing.co.uk
Web: www.pitchpublishing.co.uk

First published 2010
Reprinted 2018

A catalogue record for this book is available from the British Library.

10-digit ISBN: 1-9054117-0-7
13-digit ISBN: 978-1-9054117-0-2

Printed and bound in India by Replika Press

To Sarah, with much love.
Thanks for putting up with it all!

FOREWORD BY JEREMY GOSS

It's difficult to believe that it is approaching 20 years now that a Norwich City team that I was so proud to be a part of, started the very first FA Premier League season with that 4-2 win at Arsenal. We had, as usual, been written off by anyone and everyone before the season started, and, maybe at half-time in that game, with us 2-0 down, there were already a few people who were not only already condemning us to relegation, but also wondering how many goals Arsenal would score in the second half?

As everyone now knows, Mike Walker brought Mark Robins on for his debut in the second half, and we turned the game, scoring four goals in a little under 15 minutes – and never looked back. That result might have surprised a few people, but not us. We had a great manager in Mike Walker; we were very fit, very confident, and we had belief in ourselves, not only as individual players, but as a team. We ended up finishing third in the Premier League, and qualifying for Europe the next season, when I made my own little mark, by scoring a few goals! But, it was a team effort, a combination of very good players and a positive mentality, which brought us that momentum and success.

We were striving to live up to the Norwich City sides of the past, great teams and players that had represented the club and earned recognition and success long before we had our time in the sun. In this book, Ed has brought together many, many moments of Norwich City history.

Great players, matches, games and incidents that will never be forgotten – and maybe some that should be! All are part of the make-up of this great club, and make an entertaining and very enjoyable read, whether you are a Norwich fan or not. I recommend it very highly and hope that you enjoy reading it and learning more about the Canaries as much as I did.

Jeremy Goss
Norwich City FC
1983-1996

ACKNOWLEDGEMENTS

In writing this book, I have lived through countless emotions – ecstatic highs and painful lows; ups, downs, laughter, tears and anger, as well as brief moments of euphoria, interrupted only by longer bouts of depression and lost hope. Such is the lot of the Norwich City supporter, who can live all of those over a period of time. Whether that encompasses many years of loyal support – or, as is quite possible, throughout the ninety minutes of just one game – or about ninety eight minutes, if it's at Old Trafford.

But I wouldn't trade it, nor any of those moments for anything, least of all the repetitive library of bland success that comprises the diet of many a football supporter in these days of instant success and gratification where despair might be the fact that the half-time Pimm's is a little off, not that your club might go out of business. Neither would, I suspect, those people involved with and close to the club who have helped me with this book.

Special thanks, therefore to Norwich City FC for all of their help, support, and co-operation, especially Will Hoy and Peter Rogers. Thanks also to Jeremy Goss for his help and wonderful insights into his time at the club.

With regard to my research, then infinite thanks are due to John Eastwood and Mike Davage for their seminal history of the club, *Canary Citizens*; also to Rob Hadgraft, author of *Norwich City: The Modern Era*, and Gareth James for this books' companion in arms *Norwich City: On This Day*.

The Premiership league table shown on page 84 is reproduced with the permission of *Football Data Co Ltd*.

Further thanks are due to Antony Last and Tim Allman of Capital Canaries; Janet Lake, Russell Saunders and Nigel Nudds. I also want to mention the late Trevor Saunders, a true gentleman and fan, whose generosity on so many occasions saw me attending Norwich matches that I would normally not have been able to attend.

Finally, thank you to Dan Tester of Pitch Publishing for guiding this book along the way, and for his constant and ever-willing help, advice, and patience. With regard to the latter, a perfect quality for any Norwich City fan!

INTRODUCTION

The *Norwich City Miscellany* is a varied collection of facts, figures, incidents and events related to the club and have occurred at various points throughout its history. It is, therefore, very gratifying that, upon bringing my work and research on this book to a close, to bathe in the warm feeling that footballing success brings, an all too rare trophy and the consequent begrudging recognition (if not admiration!) that has followed in the national media.

Norwich City have crowned their 2009/10 season by becoming League One (the 'old' Third Division) champions, the first time at that level since 1935, when we topped the old Division Three (South), pipping Coventry City to the title by an impressive seven-point margin. For those that wish to correct me, yes, we did win promotion from Division Three in 1960, but that was 'only' as runners-up!

The 2009/10 season as a whole has seen a lot of new statistics thrown up for fans of the club to devour. The Canaries finished the season with 95 points, their highest-ever league tally. Of the 46 league games played, the Canaries won 29 of them; with 12 of those victories in away games – two more club records beaten. The club broke a further record in winning eleven consecutive home league games.

Meanwhile, captain Grant Holt became the first player to score 30 goals for Norwich in all competitions since Ron Davies did exactly the same in 1963/64. It has been a season of rare success and achievement for the club, and one worth celebrating. However, for me, and countless others, the celebration is in the club itself and every aspect of its history. Matches won and lost; great players and managers; moments of joy and sorrow (can you ever "treat those two imposters just the same"?); financial worries and uncertainty; frustration; despair… and hope, always hope. Hope is a priceless asset for any football fan and it exists in abundance throughout Norwich City and its supporters, all over the world. We all hope for the best, and the best is what we always hope for.

This book is about some of those moments for celebration. My hope is that you enjoy it.

Edward Couzens-Lake

CLUB ORIGINS

THE first known recorded reference about football in Norwich occurred in the *Norfolk Chronicle* on December 19th 1868, under the heading of 'Norwich Football Club'. The article mentioned that the club had already begun to play matches at the Norfolk and Norwich cricket ground, where members met weekly on every Tuesday and Thursday during the winter months. The club soon attracted upwards of 30 members, but was "...still open to gentlemen who, having been proposed by a member will send in their names to the secretary for the approval of the committee..." However, despite the article going on to say that they hoped "...to hear of some foot-ball matches before the close of the season...", later reports on those matches suggested that these games and the club itself was not playing football of the association type, but something more approaching rugby, with talk of "touchdowns" and "kicking tries". Rugby football, or a variant of, seemed, therefore, to be more popular in Norwich at the time than association football, although even this early club was not successful or prominent in the long term, and it is thought to have gone out of existence four years after its formation. Norwich City Football Club as formed on Tuesday 17th June 1902, nearly 34 years after those first tentative steps towards introducing football (of any type) to the good folk of Norwich had first been explored. The club's formation was made following a meeting at the Criterion Cafe, in White Lion Street, Norwich. The meeting was reported in the following day's edition of the *Eastern Daily Press*. The gentleman (for such pursuits at time were strictly for gentlemen) who eventually became the first chairman of the club, a Mr Robert Webster, is quoted as saying that there had been "...a great agitation for the support of a Norwich City team..." He had certainly caught the mood of his contemporaries, and later on in the meeting, when the Rev H. Wimble stated that he was glad to hear of the formation of the club, he was "...loudly cheered..." Clearly heartened by this response, the Rev Wimble seized the opportunity for a little fire and brimstone, stating that he "...wanted to brighten the life of the villages by forming football teams all over the country...", indeed, "...let them have as many teams as possible all over the country...". Fortunately, the meeting had no such lofty aspirations, and stuck to its goal (pun intended) of forming just the one club, thus the Canaries came to be hatched.

CHAMPIONSHIP GLORY!

THE famous Football League Championship trophy that has previously been shared around clubs such as Arsenal, Liverpool, Leeds United, Manchester United and Everton was finally won by Norwich City in 2004. However, by this time, the trophy was awarded to the winners of what used to be the old Second Division, by then the Football League First Division. Oddly enough, Norwich became the very last winners of the competition in that particular guise, as the second tier of English football was renamed the Football League Championship from the 2004/05 season onwards.

CAPTAIN DRURY

THE victorious captain for Norwich City during that Championship-winning season was Adam Drury. Drury was signed for £500,000 from Peterborough United in March 2001; previous boss Barry Fry said that he was "the best left-back outside the Premiership".

PROMOTION CAPTAINS

DRURY was following in the footsteps of some very famous names at Norwich when he lifted the First Division Championship in May 2004. Norwich had previously won promotion, as champions, under the rugged leadership of Duncan Forbes in 1972, Dave Stringer (promoted in third place) in 1974, Mick McGuire (again, promoted in third place) in 1982, and, for the second time as champions, under Dave Watson in 1986.

IN THE BEGINNING

NORWICH'S first competitive season as a football club was in 1902/03, when they competed in the Norfolk and Suffolk League. Despite an excellent start to the season, which included an opening 4-2 victory over the formidable Beccles Caxton, optimism which grew after four consecutive victories was soon deflated after a 7-0 defeat to Kirkley on January 3rd 1903. The club went on to lose 9-2 to Lowestoft Town that April, swiftly redeeming themselves with a thumping 8-1 win over Lynn Town on the last day of the season, finishing that season third in that league. However, it has to be said, this was one point below runners-up, Ipswich Town.

CUP RUN KEEPERS

NORWICH City's proud tradition for having outstanding goalkeepers first came to national prominence during their epic FA Cup run in the 1958/59 season. The goalkeeper in the famous 3-0 victory at Carrow Road over Manchester United in the third round that season was Ken Nethercott. He joined Norwich as an amateur in 1947, going on to make 416 senior appearances for the club. However, due to injury sustained in the first game, the glory of Norwich's quarter-final replay success over Sheffield United and the two semi-final matches played against Luton Town was not his, but that of his understudy, Sandy Kennon. South African-born Kennon took Nethercott's place in the team and went on to make 255 appearances for the club himself, his final game being a 1-1 home draw against Newcastle United on October 31st 1964. By this time, Kennon himself was vying for first-team duties with an ambitious 24-year-old that had signed from Wrexham the previous summer, and, as memorable as both his and Nethercott's time at the club had been, one wonders if either of them expected his successor to become the most famous of the trio?

KEELAN KEELAN!

THAT man was Kevin Damien Keelan (MBE). He made his first appearance for Norwich City on August 24th 1963, remaining more or less a regular feature in the side once the position became his own in November of the following year. Keelan's career with the Canaries spanned three decades, his last appearance for the club being a particularly memorable one, as it was the famous 5-3 home defeat to Liverpool on February 9th 1980, the game that is most famous for a spectacular volleyed goal from Justin Fashanu. That goal and the match itself have long since eclipsed the fact that it was Keelan's last game, but what tremendous service he gave the club. In all, he made 673 appearances for Norwich, including playing a remarkable 133 consecutive league games between August 1971 and September 1974. During a particularly good period of form at the club, then Norwich manager John Bond is said to have rejected an approach from Manchester United for Keelan's services, allegedly saying that he didn't think Keelan "would be interested" in the move! Keelan became an inaugural member of the Norwich City Hall of Fame in 2002.

FA CUP SEMI-FINALS

NORWICH have never won the FA Cup, or reached the final of the competition. However, they have played in three semi-finals. The first was the culmination of that splendid FA Cup run of 1958/59, when the clash with Luton Town went to a replay after a 1-1 draw at White Hart Lane, a game played in front of nearly 64,000 supporters. The replay, played four days later on March 18th 1959 saw Norwich go down 1-0, future Northern Ireland manager Billy Bingham scoring. It was to be 30 years before Norwich would get to the semi-final stage again, losing, again by 1-0, to Everton on April 15th 1989, Pat Nevin scoring the winner at Villa Park on a day when the other semi-final, between Liverpool and Nottingham Forest, will always be remembered for the Hillsborough tragedy. Norwich made short work of getting to their third FA Cup semi-final, doing so again in 1992, when Sunderland were the opponents at Hillsborough, the first time the stadium had been used as a neutral ground since that fateful day. Norwich were marginal favourites to defeat Sunderland, however, with striker Robert Fleck not having fully recovered from injury, the Canaries lacked the attacking guile that had characterised their season, and, again lost 1-0. John Byrne scored the decisive goal.

SWEET FA

THE club's more recent FA Cup adventures since then have often featured Norwich as the would-be 'giant' in danger of being eliminated themselves. The Canaries were the focus of the nation's attention in November 2009, when their first-round tie at non-league Paulton Rovers was televised live by ITV. Pundits and viewers hoping for a Paulton victory were disappointed, however, as Norwich convincingly won, 7 0. In 2007, Norwich faced another non league side, this time Tamworth. The BBC broadcast the game live. There were no shocks to be had here either, Norwich winning 4-1, Dion Dublin and Darren Huckerby scoring a brace apiece. It wasn't always plain sailing for Norwich against supposedly 'inferior' opposition in the competition though. Then non-league Dagenham & Redbridge gave the Canaries a scare at Carrow Road in a fourth-round tie in 2003, Zema Abbey's stoppage-time goal sealing a perhaps undeserved 1-0 win for Norwich against a side who had more than matched them over the 90 minutes.

PICK A BONE

SCOTTISH international striker Jimmy Bone has the distinction of scoring the Canaries' first goal in the top division of English football, netting the Norwich goal in their 1-1 draw against Everton on August 12th 1972. Bone played just 39 games for the club, scoring nine goals, before joining Sheffield United in 1973, a deal that saw fiery Welsh midfielder Trevor Hockey join Norwich in part exchange.

FIRST FIRST DIVISION TEAM

THE Norwich City team that Ron Saunders picked for that first-ever top-flight game against Everton at Carrow Road was as follows: 1. Kevin Keelan, 2. Clive Payne, 3. Geoff Butler, 4. Dave Stringer, 5. Duncan Forbes, 6. Max Briggs, 7. Doug Livermore, 8. Jimmy Bone, 9. David Cross, 10. Graham Paddon, 11. Terry Anderson, 12. Neil O'Donnell. Of that twelve, only Keelan played in all 42 league games, whilst the twelfth man on that day, Neil O'Donnell, was an unused substitute for the Canaries on 25 occasions.

PADDON HUMBLES ARSENAL

PERHAPS Norwich's most famous moment during their inaugural First Division season came in the League Cup. On December 21st 1972, the Canaries travelled to Highbury to play Arsenal in a fifth-round tie, stunning the home crowd of nearly 38,000 fans with an unlikely 3-0 victory; Graham Paddon scoring a hat-trick. A left-sided midfielder, Paddon's performances for Norwich led to speculation he might become the first player to be selected for England while at the club. Paddon joined West Ham United in late 1973, as part of the deal that brought Ted McDougall to Norwich. He returned to City in November 1976, and made 340 league appearances for the club in all.

NARROW ESCAPE

NORWICH finished in 20th place at the end of that season. Crystal Palace and West Bromwich Albion, who finished beneath them, were relegated. Norwich thus have the dubious honour of being the last top-flight side to avoid relegation by finishing third from bottom, as the 'three up, three down' promotion and relegation rule was introduced for the very next season.

DEFENSIVE HOLES IN BLACKBURN, LANCASHIRE

ON October 3rd 1992, Premiership leaders Norwich City travelled to Blackburn Rovers in what was expected to be a close game between two of the division's leading teams – and lost 7-1! It is one of nine times Norwich have conceded seven goals on their travels, a total of two 7-0s, six 7-1s and one 7-3. The loss at Blackburn set a record that still stands today; it is the heaviest defeat any team leading the top division of England have suffered going into a game in that lofty position. Despite the Blackburn defeat, Norwich ended that Premiership season in third place, and qualified for Europe, ending the season with a negative goal difference, establishing another unlikely record; the highest-ever finishing team to have achieved that statistic.

DRAW THAT FELT LIKE A WIN

NORWICH have been involved in nine 4-4 draws, three of those coming at Carrow Road. Perhaps the most remarkable one of all was the home Premiership game against Middlesbrough on January 22nd 2005. 4-1 down, with less than ten minutes remaining, Hasselbaink scoring the fourth in the 78th minute with a degree of arrogance that suggested the visitors were bored with their prey and wanted to go home. Perhaps that was their undoing? In the 80th minute, Dean Ashton made the score a little more respectable, but, as stoppage time approached, defeat seemed inevitable until Leon McKenzie latched on to a Huckerby cross to make it 4-3 and another assist for Huckerby. Finally, in the dying seconds, Norwich salvaged a point when the most unlikely of scorers, Adam Drury, popped into the penalty area to head home a Huckerby corner. Drury's point-saving goal was only his third in a Norwich career that now spans well over 300 matches.

GOALS A'PLENTY

COLCHESTER United manager Paul Lambert was a happy man following the first league games of the 2009/10 season, as his team led the embryonic League One table following a 7-1 victory at Norwich. It certainly made the powers-that-be at Carrow Road sit up and take note. Following the swift sacking of manager Bryan Gunn after that result, they appointed Paul Lambert as the new Canaries manager.

MARTIN PETERS

NORWICH are part of a very select band of just nine English clubs that have had a player on their books who has scored in a FIFA World Cup Final (up to 2010). Peters was signed from Tottenham Hotspur by John Bond for just £50,000 in March 1975, going on to make 232 appearances for Norwich (more than he made for Tottenham, the club he is most closely associated with) scoring 50 goals. Tottenham clearly thought that his career was on the wane when he was sold to Norwich, even though, at the time, Peters was only 31. So exceptional were his performances for the club, that there was talk of an England recall – that never came – but he did prove his doubters at White Hart Lane wrong if age and form had been questioned, playing in all of Norwich's league matches in the 1975/76 and 1976/77 seasons, scoring 17 goals, becoming club captain following the departure of Duncan Forbes. He won the club's 'Player of the Year' award in both of those seasons. Of those 17 goals, one remains strongly in the memory... It's December 10th 1977 and Norwich are 1-0 up against league champions Liverpool. Attacking the Barclay End, a Norwich attack is thwarted by a defensive Emlyn Hughes header which only goes as far as Colin Suggett, who laid the ball off to Jimmy Neighbour on the Norwich left. Neighbour's cross is met by Phil Neal, who narrowly beat Roger Gibbins to the ball, which is cleared. Then, from nowhere (Peters' nickname was 'The Ghost'), arriving on the edge of the D is Peters, who hit the ball first time on the volley, right footed, giving England goalkeeper Ray Clemence no chance at all. Peters strides to take the acclaim of the fans in the Barclay End, both arms aloft, already a Norwich City legend. Peters became a hugely influential figure at the club, his knowledge an example to the younger players, amongst them, Kevin Reeves and Justin Fashanu. Peters admits that he left Norwich too early, accepting a position as player-coach at Sheffield United in the summer of 1980, admitting at a later date, that he had made a mistake and should have stayed at Carrow Road. Perhaps it was not surprising that Peters felt such a strong bond with the area, his attraction to Norfolk had been with him at an early age when family holidays were spent in the county, one which now affectionately regards him as one of 'its own'.

MARTIN PETERS

BAYERN SUNK

NORWICH'S famous 2-1 victory over Bayern Munich in the first leg of their second-round Uefa Cup tie in October 1993 is often quoted as the only time that an English club has won at Bayern's famous Olympic Stadium. Perhaps what is more impressive is that Norwich were the first club to defeat Bayern Munich at that ground in European competition. Goals from Jerry Goss and Mark Bowen sealed the Norwich victory, with Christian Nerlinger pulling one back for the hosts just before half-time.

I'LL DRINK TO THAT!

NORWICH signed Kevin Drinkell from Grimsby Town for £105,000 in June 1985. Drinkell was seen as an essential signing if Norwich were to recover from relegation the previous season and go straight back up into Division One. It took him six league games to open his Canary account, netting a brace in Norwich's convincing 4-0 Carrow Road win over Sheffield United on September 7th, a game that was attended by just 12,899 spectators. He scored in the following two matches too and ended up leading marksman for the Canaries at the end of the season, scoring 22 goals in 41 league games. A formidable striking partnership with John Deehan never quite came to fruition, however, partially because of a run of games that saw Deehan slot in at left-back. After City's promotion, Drinkell adapted to life in top flight football well, scoring his first goal in a 4-3 win over Southampton at Carrow Road on August 30th 1986. He ended the season with 19 goals from 42 league and cup games, the only league ever-present.

CANARY RANGERS

DRINKELL was one of two Norwich players to join Glasgow Rangers under the watchful eye of Graeme Souness in the 1980s, departing Norwich for Glasgow in June 1988 for £600,000. Two years earlier, Canaries keeper Chris Woods had trod the same path, signing for a similar fee. The Scottish giant's over-the-border raids on Norfolk didn't stop with the departure of Souness, however, with Walter Smith paying the Carrow Road outfit £1.2m for Dale Gordon in 1991. All three players are members of the Norwich City Hall of Fame.

FAMOUS FANS

NO journalist on earth can resist adding a sly cooking pun when writing a story about Norwich. This is because of the club's well known affiliation with TV chef Delia Smith, who, along with her husband Michael Wynn-Jones, are the club's majority shareholders. However, Norwich City can boast some other 'famous' fans, one of the most well known being actor, presenter and raconteur Stephen Fry, singer Cathy Dennis, TV presenter David Frost and ex-*Blue Peter* presenter and Sky Sports anchorman Simon Thomas. HRH Prince Andrew is also rumoured to be a Canaries fan, but has yet to be seen at any matches!

DELIA COOKS UP A STORM!

SEE, I'm doing it now! Delia's support and love for the club was never more aptly illustrated than when she came onto the Carrow Road pitch at half-time during a match against Manchester City on February 28th 2005. Having gone 2-0 up, Norwich had been pegged back to 2-2, and it was all too much for Delia. Grabbing a microphone, she stood in the centre circle and uttered those 28 words which have gone down into Carrow Road folklore; "...a message to the best football supporters in the world... we need a 12th man here... where are you? WHERE ARE YOU? Let's be 'aving you... come on!.." Sadly, her admirable and passionate stance – which she later admitted had been completely spontaneous – had little effect on fans or team and Norwich went on to lose the match 3-2.

IS DELIA AN IPSWICH FAN?

DELIA was a regular on kids' TV programme *Swap Shop* in the late 1970s, and it was in her guise as presenter – and someone who lived nearby – that she was sent to Ipswich on the morning of their 1978 FA Cup Final date with Arsenal, supposedly as a 'celebrity Ipswich fan', seen wearing an Ipswich rosette and scarf! She has strongly denied any patronage towards the blue tribe across the border ever since and claims that she only appeared as such, because the BBC had instructed her to as part of the feature – such was the terrible price that one had to pay to appear on TV at that time. Delia later admitted that she had worn her Norwich scarf underneath the Ipswich one!

TRANSFERS

THE record transfer fee paid for a player is £3.5 million to West Bromwich Albion for Welsh international striker Robert Earnshaw in January 2006. Earnshaw was signed to replace Dean Ashton, sold for a record fee of £7.25 million to West Ham United that month. Ashton had previously been Norwich's record buy, when the Canaries signed him from Crewe Alexandra for £3 million in January 2005. The record purchase prior to him was Jon Newsome, a strong and hugely underrated centre-back who was the club's first £1 million signing when he joined from Leeds United in July 1994.

SUTTON WHO?

PRIOR to Ashton's departure, Norwich's record transfer fee received was the £5 million paid by Blackburn Rovers for striker Chris Sutton in July 1994 – the first time such a fee had been paid by an English club. Sutton was an unknown when he broke into the team in 1991 – initially as a centre-half. He scored 43 goals in 127 games for City and went on to win a Premiership winner's medal with Blackburn. He also played for Celtic and Chelsea.

BARGAIN BASEMENT

NEVER mind all the big fees, Norwich have also come up with some absolute transfer steals in their history. Few would argue that the £50,000 paid to Tottenham for World Cup winner Martin Peters in 1975 was not value for money, nor the £100,000 paid to Aberdeen for goalkeeper Bryan Gunn in 1986. When David Williams joined the club from Bristol Rovers for just £40,000 in 1985, very few Norwich fans had even heard of the 30-year old Welsh midfielder, but he was a skilful and popular player who went on to make 74 appearances and play for his country.

SELLING CLUB

NORWICH have long had a reputation for selling on their best players, but it is not a modern trait. Back in 1935, Arsenal noted the potential of outside-right Alf Kirchen, and made City an offer of £6,000, which the club could not refuse. Kirchen had played just 18 games for Norwich – but had scored 10 goals – hence Arsenal's timely move.

PHELAN GOOD

MANCHESTER United assistant manager Mike Phelan played 194 times for Norwich between 1985 and 1989, scoring ten goals, including a memorable opener in the Canaries' 2-1 win at Old Trafford on October 26th 1988.

MIKE BASSETT – NORWICH MANAGER

BEFORE his controversial stint as England manager, fictional boss Mike Bassett led Norwich to glory in the Mr Clutch Cup. Footage of the victorious Norwich team parading the trophy had to be filmed in St. Albans, as Norwich City Council would not grant the production company permission to film in Norwich!

PETER GRANTED

PRIOR to his short spell as Norwich manager in 2006/07, Scottish midfielder Peter Grant played for the Canaries between 1997 and 1999, making 68 appearances and scoring three goals. Norwich boss Mike Walker had previously tried to sign him from Celtic in 1992, but Grant turned down the move at that time, preferring to extend his career at Parkhead.

A BRAZILIAN FIRST

BORN in Brazil in the late 1890s, Norwich outside-right Edward Laxton was the first Brazilian-born player to play in English football. His debut coincided with Norwich's first league match, a 1-1 draw at Plymouth Argyle on August 28th 1920. Laxton made 38 Southern League and Division Three appearances for Norwich, scoring one goal.

CARROW ROAD'S RECORD

THE record attendance at Carrow Road, one that is likely to stand for all time, is 43,984 for an FA Cup quarter-final match against Leicester City on March 30th 1963. Norwich lost 2-0. The next home game, a league match against Chelsea a week later, saw a crowd of just 20,205 witness a fine 4-1 win, Jimmy Hill (no, not that one) scoring two of the goals.

EFAN STRIKES

NIGERIAN striker Efan Ekoku was not at Norwich for very long but, during his stay at the club from 1993 to 1995, he certainly played his part, cementing not only a club landmark, but a Premiership one as well. In September 1993 he scored the club's first-ever goal in competitive European football in the 3-0 Carrow Road victory over Dutch side Vitesse Arnhem in the Uefa Cup first round. Less than a fortnight later he scored four goals as the Canaries thumped Everton 5-1 at Goodison Park. This made Ekoku the first player in the Premiership to score four goals in a match. In all, Ekoku scored a total of 17 goals in 45 appearances for Norwich before becoming another example of the club's financial need to sell their best players when he joined then fellow Premiership side Wimbledon for a fee approaching £1 million.

O'NEILL CHASED AWAY?

NORWICH did seem to have an infuriating habit of losing good players in the 1990s; this also extended to letting one of the most respected managers in the modern game slip between their fingers too. Martin O'Neill, under the tutelage of Brian Clough at Nottingham Forest, won a European Cup winner's medal, as well as commence a 64-game playing career with Northern Ireland, which included the 1982 World Cup finals. He is best known now for his managerial stints at Leicester City, Celtic and Aston Villa. Indeed, many football writers, when cataloguing his career in management neglect (or forget!) the brief spell he had in charge at Carrow Road, following his joining the club from Wycombe Wanderers in 1995. O'Neill took over a club that had just been relegated from the Premiership, and led a Canaries side that included the likes of Darren Eadie, Robert Fleck, and Danny Mills to some encouraging early results. However, O'Neill was rumoured to be at loggerheads with Norwich chairman Robert Chase over team strengthening, and reportedly resigned as manager after Chase had refused to sanction a move for the then Hull City striker Dean Windass. Ironically, O'Neill quit the club just hours before Norwich were due to play his next club, Leicester City, a game the Canaries lost 3-2, having been 2-0 up, future Norwich player Iwan Roberts scoring the Leicester equaliser. O'Neill had been at Norwich for barely five months.

IWANNNN!

WELSH international striker Iwan Roberts signed for Norwich from Wolves for £850,000 in July 1997. He found the early going a little tough, taking some terrace stick at Norwich, and struggled to score goals. Coming back from a niggling injury he scored the first of 96 goals for the club with a trademark header in a 3-1 home defeat by Middlesbrough on November 15th 1997. His 95th and 96th (and final) goals for Norwich came in the 3-1 win at Crewe Alexandra on May 9th 2004, the last day of the old First Division season. Norwich were already champions when the game commenced; the first of those two goals came from a twice-taken penalty.

LEADING GOALSCORER – TOTAL

THE all-time goalscoring record for Norwich is held by outside-right Johnny Gavin who totalled 132 goals in 338 appearances for the Canaries from 1948/54 and 1955/58. Gavin was signed from Limerick City for just £1,500 in August 1948. Following his retirement from the game, Gavin had a spell working as a publican, as well as painting and decorating!

LEADING GOALSCORER – SEASON

RALPH Hunt holds the record for the most goals scored in one season by a Norwich player, netting 33 times in 48 games in the 1955/56 season. He was the club's leading goalscorer the following season as well – scoring 21 in 43 – achieving that in an otherwise poor Norwich side that finished five points adrift at the bottom of the old Division Three (South) table.

MACDOUGALL AND BOYER

TED MacDougall and Phil Boyer formed perhaps the best known Norwich City striking partnership. Between them, they scored 84 goals in the 1974/75 and 1975/76 seasons. Of the two, MacDougall was the more prolific goalscorer, claiming two hat-tricks in four games in 1975, the first coming in a 5-3 Carrow Road win over Aston Villa on August 23rd, the second in another home win, the 4-2 romp against Everton just a fortnight later. Boyer scored some vital goals, one example being the equaliser in the 1-1 draw against Manchester United on March 17th 1976.

CANARIES PLAYING FOR ENGLAND

NORWICH have had six players picked for England whilst they were on the books at Carrow Road. The first was Phil Boyer, who made his first, and only, appearance under the management of Don Revie in March 1976, as England defeated Wales 2-1 at Wembley. Kevin Reeves followed, his sole appearance coming in a 2-0 Wembley victory over Bulgaria in 1979 – a game which also saw Glenn Hoddle make his England debut. Mark Barham followed, becoming the first Norwich player to make more than one appearance for England – his two England caps both coming against Australia in England's low key 1983 tour – playing the full 90 minutes in the 0-0 draw on June 12th and England's 1-0 victory three days later. Dave Watson became the fourth Norwich player in 1984, making six appearances in total and consequently becoming the club's most capped England player. Goalkeeper Chris Woods followed a year later, and it is worth noting that, when Dave Watson came on as a substitute in England's match against the USA on June 16th 1985 (England won 5-0), it was the first and only time, to date, Norwich City had more than one player appearing for England, Chris Woods making his full debut in the same match. Watson's own England debut had been in England's famous 2-0 victory over Brazil at the Maracana. Twenty years then elapsed until the sixth, and final (to date) Norwich player made an England appearance; goalkeeper Robert Green coming on as a second-half substitute in England's 3-2 victory over Colombia in the USA in 2005.

MOST CAPPED PLAYER

WELSH full-back Mark Bowen is Norwich's most capped player, appearing 35 times for Wales in a career with the Canaries that lasted for nine years. Bowen signed from Tottenham Hotspur for just £90,000 in July 1987, making 399 appearances and scoring 27 goals. He would undoubtedly have made 400 appearances and many more for the club, but was dropped following perceived criticism of then-manager Gary Megson's tactics. He subsequently left the club on a free transfer, and joined West Ham United. Bowen's finest moment as a Norwich player was almost certainly the club's famous 2-1 Uefa Cup win over Bayern Munich, his 29th-minute looping header prompting BBC commentator John Motson to excitedly claim, "… and Norwich are two up! This is almost fantasy football!"

MARK BOWEN

THE FRIENDLY CUP FINAL

THE 1985 League Cup Final between Norwich and Sunderland revives fond memories for many Canaries fans who were at Wembley on that damp April day. Both sets of supporters seemed intent on enjoying the occasion as much as possible, and this was initially evident some hours before kick-off when an impromptu football match was held between the fans of the two teams in the Wembley car park – about "fifty a side" according to one eyewitness. During the build-up to the game, fans in the stadium, watching a display by the famous Red Devils parachute team, witnessed one team member crash onto the Wembley roof, before sliding off, and out of the stadium – luckily, he was not seriously injured. The game itself is perhaps memorable for two particular moments; Asa Hartford's deflected winning goal for Norwich early in the second half, and Clive Walker's missed penalty for Sunderland not long afterwards. Walker's penalty miss was the first in an English domestic final at Wembley. At the end of the match, Norwich squad player and former Sunderland forward Gary Rowell walked around the pitch bedecked in Norwich and Sunderland scarves, receiving cheers of support from all over the still packed terraces. Later on, outside the ground, Norwich and Sunderland fans mingled freely, exchanging shirts, scarves, hats, and other mementoes of the game. The two clubs eventually agreed to mark the occasion by commissioning a trophy that they would contest whenever they played in the future, calling it the Friendly Trophy. Sunderland are the present holders of the trophy, having beaten Norwich 4-1 in a League Cup second-round tie at Carrow Road on August 24th 2009.

LEAGUE CUP LOSSES

NORWICH had previously appeared in two Wembley League Cup Finals, losing 1-0 to Tottenham Hotspur in 1973, Ralph Coates scoring the winner, and by the same scoreline in 1975, when Ray Graydon and Aston Villa saw them off. Ironically, this game, ten years before Walker's penalty miss for Sunderland, nearly saw Graydon become the first to hold that dubious honour, his penalty was tipped onto the post by Keelan before Graydon poked home the rebound. It remains the only time a senior English cup final has been played by two teams outside of the top division. Former Norwich manager Ron Saunders was, by then, in charge at Villa.

UNLUCKY O'NEILL

NORTHERN Irish international John O'Neill signed from QPR in December 1987 as a replacement for Manchester United-bound Steve Bruce. On his debut against Wimbledon he collided with ex-Canary John Fashanu, after only 34 minutes, rupturing knee ligaments. He never recovered from the injury and later had to quit the game, hence establishing an unenviable record of having one of the shortest playing spells of any Norwich player.

STEVE THE BRUCE

STEVE Bruce signed from Gillingham for £135,000 ahead of the 1984/85 season, and made an immediate impact, scoring an own goal on his debut against Liverpool. He redeemed himself by scoring at the right end, to help earn the Canaries a 3-3 draw. He made 180 appearances, scoring 21 goals, including that header against Ipswich in the 1985 League Cup semi-final.

BECKHAM THE CANARY?

DAVID Beckham spent a week training at Norwich in 1987. Needless to say, he impressed during his time at the club and was asked if he would like to sign for Norwich by then youth team coach Kit Carson. Sadly, the 11-year-old Becks had, by this time, already agreed to sign for Manchester United.

BAKERO IN AND OUT

SPANISH international and one-time Barcelona legend and European Cup winner Jose Maria Bakero spent some time with Norwich following his release from Barcelona in 1997. Despite his pedigree and experience, Bakero did not impress Norwich manager Mike Walker, and was soon on his travels again. City later went on to sign Peter Grant from Celtic instead.

"GIVE IT TO VARCO"

A POPULAR terrace chant at Norwich when Cornwall-born Percy Varco was at the club. Varco scored in 7 of his first 8 games at Norwich, following his move from QPR in 1927. An impressive 47 goals in 65 games followed, including netting on both his debut and final appearance.

THE NEST

HOW appropriate that the home for the Canaries prior to their move to Carrow Road in 1935 was The Nest, a disused quarry in Rosary Road. It's most distinguishing feature was perhaps the large concrete wall at one end of the ground, supporting a cliff, upon which supporters would watch matches. Before even the pitch could be laid however, the club had to move thousands of tons of earth, before taking down the structures from their first home, at Newmarket Road and transporting them, by horse and cart, across the city. The task was completed in time for the commencement of the 1908/09 season, and The Nest saw its first match on September 1st, a 1-1 friendly against Fulham in front of just over 3,000 people. Following 4-0 and 10-2 defeats in their opening Southern League fixtures, the first competitive game at the ground saw Norwich stop the early season rot with a 0-0 draw against Portsmouth.

FLOWN THE NEST

BY 1935, it became clear that the growth and ambitions of the club were outgrowing The Nest. In addition, letters were received from the FA questioning The Nest's suitability for staging matches, especially as crowds in excess of 22,000 had been recorded for home matches against Newport in April 1934 – just five years earlier, the maximum crowds had been just 10,000. Second Division status, attained as Division 3 (South) champions in 1934, made the need for a move essential. Work started on the new site, alongside the River Wensum in June 1935, and the whole construction, said to be the largest the city had seen since the building of Norwich Castle in 1067, was completed in just 82 days!

CARROW ROAD

THE new ground was named after the ancient Carrow Abbey which stood on the southern bank of the River Wensum. Following that 4-3 win over West Ham United in the first game at the new ground, City then had a bad run of results, losing their next seven league games, before a thumping 4-2 home win over Port Vale. The biggest crowd for that inaugural Carrow Road season was 32,378, for an FA Cup third-round tie against Chelsea on January 11th 1936 that ended 0-0.

LIVE AND EXCLUSIVE

NORWICH'S first-ever live TV game was the 1-0 win over Sunderland in the 1985 League Cup Final win, televised by the BBC with John Motson commentating. Their first live league match was the 2-1 victory over West Ham United on December 27th 1988, shown on ITV, the victory keeping Norwich at the top of the First Division table. The club's first live TV date in the Premiership was a 3-1 home victory over Nottingham Forest on August 31st 1992, goals from Ian Crook, David Phillips and Lee Power securing the three points, which, again, maintained their place at the top of the early Premiership table.

EUROPE!

THE Canaries' debut in European football, the 3-1 victory over Vitesse Arnhem in September 1993, was not shown live on any British channel, but anyone who had cable TV at the time could view it live on Dutch TV.

FASH BASH

JUSTIN Fashanu won the BBC Goal of the Season for his stunning turn and volley during Norwich's 5-3 home defeat to Liverpool in January 1980.

UNITED'S TITLE

NORWICH'S magnificent and unlikely tilt at the Premiership title was close to its end following their (Sky TV titled) 'Premiership Decider' game against Manchester United at Carrow Road on April 5th 1993. United were 3-0 up at half-time, and, despite a second-half goal by Mark Robins, Norwich ended the game the losers and in third place, where they remained.

TAKE TWO

THE two clubs were paired together at Carrow Road on the first weekend of the following season, and Sky TV were there again, promoting the match as a clash between two Premiership title contenders. However, the game, played at a gloriously sunny Carrow Road on Sunday August 15th 1993 went United's way, Bryan Robson opening the scoring in a 2-0 victory.

MILLION POUND MAN

SIGNED for just £50,000 from Bournemouth in February 1977 after an initial loan spell, Kevin Reeves was the first in a long list of players sold by Norwich for £1 million and more. Reeves was signed by John Bond and, whilst at Norwich, became the second Norwich player to be picked for England, playing against Bulgaria in 1979. In his three years at Norwich, Reeves made 133 appearances, scoring 42 goals, playing alongside a veritable 'Who's Who' of Norwich strikers, including Roger Gibbins, Viv Busby, Martin Chivers and Davie Robb. He made his debut away at Arsenal on January 15th, and ending up being substituted and replaced by Billy Steele. Bond rested him for the following match, at home to Liverpool, but Reeves was back in the side the following week for the game against Stoke City, marking the occasion with a goal. He ended that initial season with eight goals from 21 league appearances, the club's second-highest goalscorer behind Busby on 11. The 1977/78 season saw Reeves start his first full campaign at the club as a first-choice striker, playing 37 of Norwich's league games mostly alongside Roger Gibbins. He ended the season with 12 goals from 37 league games, a little behind free-scoring full-back John Ryan who finished up on 15. By now, Reeves was starting to come to the attention of bigger clubs, that first England cap adding to the attraction. He acquitted himself for England well, and, less than 48 hours later, was playing for Norwich again, swapping Trevor Francis as his strike partner for Justin Fashanu in the league game at Manchester United. Norwich lost 5-0, which perhaps spoilt his week a little! By now, much speculation was surrounding Reeves, however, when John Bond informed him that Manchester City were, again, showing an interest (Reeves had decided against a move to the same club earlier that season), he decided to make the move, especially given that Norwich's form had slipped – they were fourth in the table going into 1980, but had fallen to 12th by March – and Manchester City had kept increasing their bid, eventually making one of £1 million that same month. Norwich accepted the offer and Reeves left, his last game being a 2-2 home draw against Brighton & Hove Albion. True to form, he scored in that match, his eighth goal that season. Furious Norwich fans subsequently protested at his departure, 'No Reeves, No Fans, No Future' banners being displayed at the next home match against West Bromwich Albion.

A SIX POINTER

NORWICH became the first club to take six points off Liverpool in one season during the 1982/83 season. A John Deehan goal gave the Canaries a 1-0 victory on December 4th, whilst, at Anfield on April 23rd, Mark Lawrenson's own goal and a Martin O'Neill effort secured a 2-0 win. Two games, two wins, three goals scored and none conceded. Not too shabby!

ANOTHER WATSON?

NORWICH signed England youth international Mark Seagraves on loan from Liverpool in November 1986, perhaps hoping he might follow in the footsteps of a previous signing from Anfield, Dave Watson. Seagraves made his debut in the 2-1 defeat at Coventry City on November 22nd, but played in just two more games for the Canaries, the last of those being a 4-0 defeat at Liverpool. Regular defender Tony Spearing was fit again for Norwich's next game at home to Arsenal, and Seagraves returned to Liverpool.

POOR AWAY DAYS

NORWICH'S disappointing league campaign of 1999/2000, which they ended in 12th place in Division One, was partly down to their poor away form. In 23 away games, the Canaries only scored 19 goals, a total beaten by Walsall and Port Vale, both of whom were relegated at the end of that season! Meanwhile, rock bottom Swindon Town secured one of only three away league victories that season at Norwich, winning 2-0 on March 22nd.

BOB SCORES

IN a playing career that took in over 300 games for Arsenal, defender Bob McNab only scored four goals. Typically, one of his strikes came in a game against Norwich, in the Gunners' 4-0 triumph at Carrow Road on September 15th 1973. He didn't get the opportunity to repeat the feat in the return game at Highbury, as he didn't play. It didn't matter as Norwich lost 2-0, both Arsenal goals coming from Alan Ball. An emerging talent for Arsenal starred on that day, a 17-year-old Liam Brady. Gunners goalkeeper Bob Wilson was no stranger to Norfolk at the time, enjoying regular breaks in Brancaster, a village on the north Norfolk coast.

PITCH AND STAGE

NORTHERN Ireland international Jim Whitley had an eight-game loan period at Norwich in August 2000. His return to Norwich nearly a decade later came on the stage of the city's Theatre Royal, where he appeared as Sammy Davis Junior in the 'Rat Pack Vegas Spectacular'.

SUPERSUB!

DAVID Fairclough made quite a reputation for himself as a regularly-scoring 'supersub' for Liverpool. However, his arrival at Norwich from Manchester City in March 1985 yielded no heroics, supersub or otherwise, as he made just two, goalless appearances for the club before joining Oldham Athletic.

NO RUSH

ONE of the more annoying facts quoted by the media in the 1980s was that Liverpool never lost when Ian Rush scored. Happily, in April 1987, Norwich rendered that fact to the history books with a 2-1 win at Carrow Road, Trevor Putney and Kevin Drinkell scoring the goals that followed Rush's opener.

THE HAREIDE HAREIDES

DEFENDER Aage Hareide was born on the Norwegian island that shares his name, although as he later pointed out, his family were named after the island, not the other way round! Hareide appeared 52 times for the Canaries before returning to Norway to play for Molde.

SAUNDERS STAYERS

WHEN Ron Saunders left Norwich in 1973, City had ten players who had made 150 or more appearances for the club. Strangely, despite his obvious faith in these players, not one of them was invited to join him at Villa Park.

GOOD GOSS!

ON the last day of the 1993/94 season, Jerry Goss scored the last goal in front of the famous Kop terrace at Anfield earning, the Canaries a 1-0 victory.

JEREMY GOSS

AT THE RACES

FAMOUS racehorse trainer Mike Channon's illustrious playing career included a memorable stint at Norwich from 1982 to 1985, seeing him score 25 goals in 112 games; he also won a League Cup winners' medal in 1985.

OOPS!

FOLLOWING Norwich's second-leg win over Ipswich in the 1985 League Cup semi-final that sealed the club's Wembley appearance, the local radio station took the opportunity to visit the winning dressing room during the post-match celebrations. It was Channon's distinctive Hampshire burr that was heard on BBC Radio Norfolk, as his comments to teammate Asa Hartford ("…you ol' bastard 'artford…") went out live on air, prompting a swift apology from Channon himself in a more restrained voice!

HARTFORD

ASA Hartford was Channon's fellow veteran sidekick at the time, his deflected shot in that 1985 League Cup Final against Sunderland giving Norwich victory. Hartford, who famously had a move to Don Revie's all-conquering Leeds United called off because of an alleged heart problem, joined Norwich in November 1984, and, despite only staying at the club for the remainder of that season, made his mark with five goals in 40 games.

VERSUS MANCHESTER UNITED

NORWICH'S first-ever competitive match against Manchester United was in an FA Cup second round match in February 1906, the Canaries being on the wrong end of a 2-0 defeat. The clubs didn't meet again for nearly 30 years. The next fixture, again, saw Norwich lose, this time by 5-0 at Old Trafford in a League Division Two game in September 1934. Their first victory came in the following February, with Alf Kirchen, Jack Vinall and Cecil Russell scoring in a 3-2 success at Carrow Road. In total, the clubs have met 58 times, in Football League and cup matches, Norwich winning 15, Manchester United 30, with 13 draws. City enjoyed a good run against Manchester United in the 1980s; in 14 league games between April 1983 and January 1990, Norwich won six, with four draws and three defeats.

PETER THE GREAT

TOTTENHAM and England striker Peter Crouch had a successful loan period at Norwich during their Championship-winning season of 2003/04. Joining from Aston Villa in September 2003, Crouch made 15 appearances, scoring four goals, including the opener on his debut, a 2-0 Carrow Road victory over Burnley.

CROSSING THE DIVIDE

DESPITE the great rivalry between the clubs, 18 different players have represented both Norwich City and Ipswich Town. Perhaps the most notorious 'double agent' is goalkeeper Andy Marshall who left Norwich on a Bosman free transfer in order to join Ipswich in July 2001.

PLAYERS NAMED!

THOSE 18 players who have played for Norwich City, as well as that team in Suffolk, are as follows: Clive Baker, Matthew Bates, Bobby Bell, Keith Bertschin, John Deehan, Louie Donowa, Allenby Driver, Alan Lee, Arran Lee-Barrett, Kevin Lisbie, Andy Marshall, Johnny Miller, Peter Morris, Trevor Putney, Jack Roy, Clive Woods, David Wright, and David Healy.

JACK WHO?

SOUTHAMPTON-born Robin 'Jack' Roy has the distinction of being the first player to represent both Norwich and Ipswich, joining Norwich in 1933, making 10 appearances, scoring 1 goal. He signed for Ipswich in 1946, having represented four other league clubs since departing Norwich in 1936.

CROOK CHANGES MIND

IAN Crook could have added himself to that list, signing an agreement with Ipswich in the summer of 1996, having been released by Norwich. However, on the day the Portman Road club announced his signing, returning Norwich manager Mike Walker asked Crook to rejoin the club, leading to the Canaries being fined for their actions.

VERSUS LIVERPOOL

FORTY-TWO years spans the first three competitive matches between Norwich and Liverpool, all in the FA Cup, and all Norwich victories. The first was a second-round tie at Anfield in February 1909, Norwich winning 3-2 with goals by J. Tomlinson, John Flanagan and Tommy Allsop. In total, 54 league and cup games have been played between the two clubs, Norwich winning 14, Liverpool 28, with 12 draws. Norwich have suffered some particularly heavy defeats at the hands of Liverpool, including a 6-2 plucking at Anfield in November 1986, Paul Walsh scoring a hat-trick for the Reds. On February 21st 1979 Liverpool won 6-0, Kenny Dalglish, David Johnson and Alan Kennedy each bagging a brace. Kevin Keelan made his last appearance of that season for Norwich that afternoon, before returning to the side at the beginning of the following campaign. Nearly a year to the day since that result, on February 9th 1980, Keelan made his last-ever appearance for Norwich City, the opponents once again being Liverpool who 'only' managed five goals on that occasion, winning 5-3. In total, Keelan played for Norwich against Liverpool on 15 occasions, letting in 30 goals, and, despite that two-goals-against-per-game average, you wonder just how many more Norwich might have conceded, had he not been in goal at the time?

SON OF THE FATHER

KENNY Dalglish's son, Paul, is one of 13 players who have played for Norwich and Liverpool. Dalglish junior joined Norwich for £300,000 from Newcastle United in May 1999, going on to make 48 appearances, scoring just two goals. Although his initial form for the club was promising, and led to regular selection for the Scotland under-21 side, he couldn't maintain it, and he eventually joined Wigan Athletic on a free transfer in 2001.

THE LUCKY THIRTEEN

PLAYERS who have represented both Norwich and Liverpool: Craig Bellamy, Peter Crouch, Paul Dalglish, David Fairclough, David Hodgson, Doug Livermore, Norman Low, Jan Molby, Jon Otsemobor, Mark Seagraves, Nick Tanner, Tony Warner and Dave Watson. Danish international midfielder Molby joined Norwich on loan in December 1995, playing five times and scoring one goal in a 2-1 League Cup defeat to Birmingham City.

HOUGHTON & CO

LEFT-sided player Harold Houghton played with distinguished company, alongside Dixie Dean whilst at Everton as well as Cliff Bastin, and one-time Norwich player Percy Varco at Exeter City. Houghton joined Norwich in March 1934 and, in a short stay at Norwich of just over 18 months, scored ten goals in 56 appearances.

ONE-GAME WONDER

GOALKEEPER John Greatrex joined Norwich as an amateur from Coventry City in 1952, but, in his six-year stay at the club only played in one game, a 3-1 home defeat against Aldershot in the last game of the 1957/58 season.

JOHN SISSONS

LEFT-winger Sissons scored for West Ham United in the 1964 FA Cup Final, at 18 becoming (and remaining) the youngest player to score in the final. He joined Norwich from Sheffield Wednesday for £30,000 in December 1973, making his debut at West Ham, his first club. Norwich lost 4-2, Ted McDougall, also playing against a former club, scoring both goals. Sissons made just 20 appearances for Norwich, scoring one goal, before signing for Chelsea.

GOLDEN OLDIE

FULL-back Albert Sturgess made his Norwich debut, against Millwall, on August 25th 1923 – at the age of 40! He remains (and will probably hold this record forever) the oldest league debutant for Norwich, retiring 53 games later at the age of 42.

WAR STOPS PLAY

DUE to play a wartime match at QPR in 1941, the Norwich team were kept back in the dressing room prior to kick off, due to the sounding of the air-raid sirens. The game was eventually abandoned.

NORWICH CITY – TOP TEN APPEARANCES

1	Kevin Keelan	673
2	Ron Ashman	662
3	Dave Stringer	499
4	Bryan Gunn	477
5	Joe Hannah	427
6	Roy McCrohan	426
7	Ian Crook	418
8	Ken Nethercott	416
9	Mark Bowen	399
10	Terry Allcock	389

KEELAN, Gunn and Nethercott were all goalkeepers. Chris Woods and Robert Green, also goalies, made 267 and 241 appearances respectively. Green's understudy for much of his time at Norwich, the admirable Paul Crichton, made just six appearances between 2001 and 2004, clearly 'suffering' because of the continual fine form of the future England keeper.

DIXIE ONE SHORT OF DOUBLE CENTURY

MARK Bowen fell one game short of making 400 competitive appearances for the club. John Deehan appeared 199 times. Signed from West Bromwich Albion in 1982 for £175,000, he scored on his debut in a 3-1 home defeat against Luton Town, and ended the following season, 1982/83 as the club's top goalscorer, claiming a total of 21 in 50 league and cup games.

MATTHEWS FINAL

HOW many of the 25,707 who attended Carrow Road for a Second Division match on March 9th 1963 were secretly hoping for a virtuoso performance from the great Stanley Matthews, making his final appearance at the ground? Matthews, whose Stoke City side won the title that season, had an off day, as Norwich won 6-0. Jim Oliver scored a hat-trick, with Gerry Mannion, Terry Allcock and Jim Conway also scoring. It was Conway's last game of that season and he went on to appear in only a further eight games for the club before joining Southend United.

INTRODUCING JOHN BOND

JOHN Bond was appointed Norwich City manager on November 25th 1973 and immediately set about changing the playing style and type of player that characterised the club. Under previous manager, Ron Saunders, Norwich had been successful winning promotion to the First Division for the first time, as well as reaching a League Cup Final. However, the football under Saunders had been questioned in some quarters, his methods tending to rely on physical effort and hard work. Bond's playing career had been influenced strongly by his time spent at West Ham United, the style and manner of their play under Ted Fenton and Ron Greenwood being something he wanted to bring to Norwich. He made an immediate impact on the playing squad, bringing in Ted McDougall from West Ham for £140,000 within a fortnight of taking the job, and, making use of his Bournemouth connections, and, despite a row between the clubs over what Bournemouth saw as player poaching, commenced bringing in players from his ex-club, amongst them, Mel Machin, Phil Boyer, Tony Powell, and, via Nottingham Forest, David Jones. Norwich were relegated at the end of that 1975/76 season, but Bond was hugely confident of them making an immediate return to the First Division the following season, and so they did, finishing third behind Manchester United and Aston Villa. His introduction of the McDougall and Boyer partnership yielded dividends that season, the duo scoring 45 league and cup goals between them. He also took Norwich to their second League Cup Final in three years. However, the club lost 1-0 to Aston Villa, the club who had finished five points ahead of them that season, and who, under the supposedly dour Saunders, had scored 79 league goals in 42 games, against the Canaries total of 58. In their first season back in the top division, Bond guided Norwich to a respectable tenth-place finish, six places above Saunders' Villa side. The Canaries had also beaten Villa 5-3 in an August league match that saw McDougall score a hat-trick. A fortnight later, Bond's exciting Canaries side beat Everton 4-2, before travelling to Burnley the following week, and, despite being 3-1 down at half-time, came back to draw 4-4, MacDougall scoring two goals. Sadly, these encouraging early years of Bond's time at Norwich did not extend to another good run in the League Cup, the club losing a second replay 6-1 to Manchester City at Stamford Bridge. Bond's, and possibly the club's, greatest signing Martin Peters scored the solitary goal.

SIGNED FOR SEVEN MILLION

WHEN Norwich signed ex-Arsenal forward Josiah 'Paddy' Sloan from Italian side Brescia in 1951, seven million was indeed the sum of money involved. However, this was in early post-war Italian Lira, and equated to about £4,000!

ON THE BALL CITY

THE Canary anthem is said to be the world's oldest football song currently still in use. However, there are claims that the song was actually written before the present Norwich City were founded in 1902, and that On The Ball City was originally composed for either Norwich Teachers or Caley's FC in the 1890s, and that Norwich CEYMS F.C, a Church club, adopted the song for themselves at that time.

THE CANARIES

NORWICH were not always referred to as The Canaries. Their original nickname was The Citizens or 'Cits', the club strip being light blue and white halved shirts. The current nickname came about in the mid-1900s, being used on a more widespread basis once the famous yellow and green playing strip was introduced in 1908.

LAMBERT'S FIRSTS

WHEN Norwich appointed Paul Lambert as manager in August 2009, they had brought to the club a man with a distinguished playing career, home and abroad. In Scotland, he won a Scottish Cup Final medal at just 17, when St. Mirren beat Dundee United in 1987. Following a move to Motherwell, Lambert joined Borussia Dortmund, becoming, in 1997, both the first British player to win a Champions League medal, as well as becoming the first British player to win a Champions League **or** European Cup winners' medal with a foreign club. He returned to Scotland with Celtic and won four Scottish Premiership titles, two Scottish Cups, and two Scottish League Cups, as well as captaining Celtic in the 2003 Uefa Cup Final.

PAUL LAMBERT

INTERNATIONAL CANARIES

SADLY, Norwich's forays into competitive European football begin and end with that Uefa Cup run in 1993/94. However, the club has often ploughed an ambitious field overseas in terms of playing friendly matches, touring Kenya in the early summer of 1975, playing five matches and winning them all, including an 8-0 win over Champion Kenya. Clearly, their hosts wanted to get their money's worth out of the Canaries, as they were due to play again the following day, this time beating Mwenge (of Mombasa) 3-1. The following pre-season, Norwich toured Norway, winning two of their three games, before heading off to Trinidad for two matches, diplomatically losing 2-0 to the President's XI but following that up a few days later by defeating the Combined Clubs XI 3-0. The next summer, 1977, saw the Canaries head out for another summer tour, this time to... Devon. They managed to lose 5-0 to Exeter City in their first game. However, the club reverted back to its jet setting ways immediately after the end of the 1977/78 season, flying off to the USA for a couple of games, which included an 11-10 shoot-out win over Tampa Bay Rowdies, whilst May 1979 saw the Canaries play seven games in 16 days on a tour to Australasia.

GOING UP!

FOLLOWING their relegation from the First Division in 1981, Norwich were strongly favoured to win promotion back to the top flight at the first attempt. Following a 1-0 home defeat to QPR on December 27th 1981, the Canaries had slumped to 12th in the table, and were only six points clear of the relegation places. A run of 11 wins in their last 14 games pushed Norwich up the table and into third place, and, although they lost their last game of the season 2-1 at Sheffield Wednesday they still remained in third place, one point ahead of the Hillsborough club, and were promoted back to the First Division, at the first attempt, for the second time. A key fixture had been the home game against Watford at the beginning of that run, back on March 13th 1982. Losing 2-1 at half-time, and given an early version of the hairdryer treatment by Ken Brown, Norwich struck back to win 4-2, goals by Dave Watson, Keith Bertschin, John Deehan and Martin O'Neill securing the win.

GOING DOWN!!!

JUST three seasons later, Norwich were relegated again, only this time the last game of the season made all the difference! The unusual thing about it is that Norwich won their last game of the season, and, following the 2-1 victory over Chelsea at a rain-soaked Stamford Bridge on May 14th 1985, City were safe in 18th place, eight points clear of Coventry City who occupied the last relegation place, in 20th position. Although Norwich had completed their fixtures, Coventry still had three to play, and, three victories from those final games would see them safe and put Norwich down. Canary fans were fairly confident. The Sky Blues only needed to lose or draw one of those three games for City to stay up. The first was at Stoke City, and maybe this was the easiest, as they had finished bottom of the table, 23 points behind Sunderland in 21st place. Coventry needed a Stuart Pearce penalty to secure a 1-0 victory. Their next game was at home to Luton Town and again Coventry toiled, securing another 1-0 victory. Their last game, however, was the ace card in the Norwich pack, home to champions Everton, who had scored 87 goals in their preceding 41 league games and had casually tossed Norwich aside in their league meeting at the end of April, winning 3-0. If Coventry could barely scrape past bottom side Stoke, then surely, surely they wouldn't beat the newly crowned league champions and send Norwich, winners of the League Cup Final at Wembley just two months earlier, back into the Second Division? Well, what do you think? Coventry thrashed an Everton side – who were clearly already thinking of the beaches of Magaluf – 4-1, and down the Canaries went. Following this (for Norwich) unfortunate end to the season, the Football League authorities changed the rules relating to league fixtures, ensuring that all of the clubs in England played their final games of the season on the same date and kick-off time. Thus, on May 3rd 1986, Norwich beat Leeds United 4-0, confirming their status as newly crowned Second Division champions and returning to Division One at the first time of asking for the third time. It had been one of the more memorable seasons in the club's history, and remains so, even today. The Canaries had the joint-best defence (along with Wimbledon) in the league, and their final goal tally of 84 was by far the highest, Kevin Drinkell finishing as top scorer with 22 goals.

DRAZEN'S NO DRAGON

IN September 1980, John Bond broke Norwich's transfer record to sign Yugoslavian international Drazen Muzinic. The £300,000 paid to Hajduk Split was thought to be a bargain and the prospect of having a man who had won a whole host of domestic honours – four league titles and five cups with Split, as well as 36 caps for Yugoslavia, including appearances at both the 1974 World Cup finals and Euro 76 – lining up alongside players like Graham Paddon, Justin Fashanu and Joe Royle understandably excited Bond. Muzinic was described as a 'utility' player, a description that is usually taken to mean he can play in a variety of positions. Sadly, for Norwich, it was more a case of him not being able to play in any position. Whilst his footballing pedigree was unquestionable, Muzinic did not settle at Norwich, and, desperately trying to find a place for him in his team, Bond played him in several roles, with Muzinic ending up wearing seven different numbered shirts (this at a time when your shirt number signified the position you played in). In all, Muzinic wore the numbers 9, 7, 4, 3, 8, 5, and (perhaps as a compromise?) the number 12. To add to the problems, Muzinic could not speak English and the club had to hire a translator from the University of East Anglia to help get the message across. Following Bond's departure, Brown commenced the 1981/82 season by giving Muzinic the left-back slot in the opening game at Rotherham United. Norwich lost 4-1 and Muzinic did not start another game until November. He played a further four league games before being substituted in Norwich's 3-1 loss at home to Luton Town. Two FA Cup appearances followed, but Brown had seen enough and in July 1982 Muzinic's contract was cancelled. It later transpired that the player had been signed without the manager having even seen him play, which led to the unforgettable quote from Justin Fashanu that the club hadn't signed Muzinic, but his milkman!

MAULED AT MILLMOOR!

DESPITE that heavy 4-1 defeat sustained at Rotherham on the first day of the 1981/82 season, Norwich still won promotion at the end of that season. The team that played against Rotherham was as follows: Woods, Barham, Muzinic, McGuire, Walford, Watson, Mendham, Shepherd, Bertschin, Paddon and Bennett; Greig Shepherd scoring for Norwich.

VANS THE MAN

A RATHER more successful Continental signing for Norwich was Dutch defender Dennis Van Wijk. Signed from Ajax in 1982, he went on to make 145 appearances for the club, scoring four goals. It was his handball in the 1985 League Cup Final against Sunderland that gave Clive Walker the chance to equalise. Walker missed, and Norwich won. Watch the highlights of the game, and look for the reaction of Norwich keeper Chris Woods when the penalty is given: it's priceless!

NICE ONE CYRIL!

BUT for World War II, Cyril Walker could have been up there with the Norwich greats. In 34 wartime friendlies for the club he scored 37 goals, eventually signing full time in 1946. However, he only played a further three games, scoring another two times.

GOSSY THE GREAT

RENOWNED for scoring spectacular goals in the successful Norwich team led by Mike Walker, Welsh international Jeremy Goss had an unusual start to his career at Norwich, initially signing on a Manpower Work Experience Scheme. Goss has since recalled that his duties at the time including running down to the local bakers to get the first-team players their sandwiches, adding, if he got it wrong, he 'got a bollocking'.

ELEMENTARY WATSON

PRIOR to signing future England international Dave Watson from Liverpool in 1980, John Bond had attempted to sign the more seasoned England centre-back by the same name from Manchester City for £100,000.

SPONSORSHIP

POLL & Withey windows became Norwich's first shirt sponsor in 1983. However, the first evidence of sponsorship at the club arrived in 1976 when Dunlop Tyres sponsored the home game against Liverpool. The Canaries failed to get a grip on the match and lost 1-0.

SHIRT SPONSORS AND MANUFACTURERS

1983-86 .... Poll & Withey Windows .... Adidas/Hummell
1986-89 .... Foster's Lager .... Hummell/Scoreline
1989-92 .... Asics .... Asics
1992-97 .... Norwich & Peterborough Building Soc .... Ribero/Mitre
1997-01 .... Colmans .... Pony/Patrick
2001-03 .... Digital Phone Company .... Xara
2003-06 .... Proton/Lotus Cars .... Xara
2006-08 .... Flybe .... Xara
2008-11 .... Aviva .... Xara

FLYBE have clearly hedged their bets in football sponsorship; as well as sponsoring the Canaries for two years, their logo has also adorned the shirts of Birmingham City, Southampton, Exeter City and Inverness Caledonian Thistle. The Ribero kit, worn by Norwich from 1992 to 1994, is regularly included in lists of worst-ever football shirts. It is unlikely that Ribero or the sponsors, the Norwich & Peterborough Building Society, were particularly bothered as this shirt coincided with the club's great Premiership and European campaign, including the Bayern Munich games. Prior to shirt sponsoring in 1983, the Canaries wore kits manufactured by Umbro and Admiral, the latter shirts, worn from 1976 to 1981 are still fondly regarded by Norwich fans and linked with the great sides managed by John Bond, and worn by players such as Martin Peters, Kevin Reeves, Kevin Keelan, and Jimmy Neighbour.

VIVA AVIVA!

FOR the Canaries' home League One fixture against Tranmere Rovers on November 14th 2009, shirt sponsors Aviva and the club arranged for the name of a charity, East Anglia's Children's Hospices (EACH) to have their name on the club strip in order to raise awareness of the charity. Norwich duly did their part, winning the game 2-0, with the shirts later sold by auction in order to raise further funds. It was the second time that Aviva had arranged for this to happen. The previous October, the Benjamin Foundation, a local charity that offers a variety of support services had been the logo on the shirt for the home game against Doncaster Rovers.

EARNIE!

ROBERT Earnshaw became Norwich's most expensive signing when he joined from West Bromwich Albion for £3.5 million on January 31st 2006. His stay at Norwich was a short one – he joined Derby County in June the following year – but his goalscoring record at the club was impressive, with 27 goals in 47 games. He would have got more had he not been out injured for much of the early part of 2007.

EUROPE

FOLLOWING the ban on English clubs playing in Europe after the Heysel tragedy in 1985, Norwich, plus the five other English clubs that missed a European place for the 1985/86 season, took part in a one-off competition in lieu of European football. Despite being in the old Second Division at the time, Norwich acquitted themselves well, beating Everton and twice drawing with Manchester United in their group, before losing 4-2 on aggregate to eventual winners Liverpool in the semi-final.

WYNTON RUFER

NORWICH'S ambitious signing of the New Zealand Young Player of the Year for 1981 and 1982 was lauded as a real coup for manager Ken Brown. However, the Home Office blocked the move and the signing fell through. Rufer has since been named New Zealand's 'Greatest-Ever Footballer' and, in a successful playing career, spent some time in the German Bundesliga at 1.FC Kaiserslautern. Needless to say, had Manchester United or Liverpool tried to sign him, there would have been no problems with a work permit at all!

STEEENOOO! STEEENOOO!

DANISH midfielder Steen Nedergaard signed from Odense in June 2000 and became one of the Canaries' most popular and versatile players. He made 97 appearances until his departure in 2003, scoring five goals, including a spectacular 25-yard effort against Coventry in March of that year.

PLAYER OF THE YEAR

THE first Norwich City player to win the club's Barry Butler Memorial Trophy was Terry Allcock in 1967. Since then, four players have won the award for two consecutive years, Kevin Keelan (1973-74); Martin Peters (1976-77); Kevin Drinkell (1986-87); and Iwan Roberts (1999-2000). Along with Steve Bruce, winner in 1985, Kevin Drinkell won the award in his first season at the club. Dion Dublin won the award in 2008, having been initially released by the club as a teenager back in 1988!

BARRY BUTLER

THE trophy has Butler's name as a tribute to the popular centre-half who wore the Norwich shirt with pride, and no lack of passion, from 1957 to 1965, making 349 appearances during that time. He was signed from Sheffield Wednesday for £5,000 in August 1957, joining as soon as his service in the RAF had ended. In 1966 he was appointed as player-coach, and an eventual role as the club's manager looked a natural progression for the Stockton-born man who had made his home in Norfolk. Tragically, he was killed in a road accident in April of that year, thus never getting the opportunity to excel, as he undoubtedly would have, in that new club role.

NEAL-Y MAN

WHEN Dave Stringer resigned as Norwich boss in 1992, ex-Liverpool and England defender Phil Neal, who had just been sacked as boss of Bolton Wanderers, was set to be appointed as his successor. However, Neal turned down the opportunity to succeed Stringer, citing a reluctance to move his family. Norwich appointed reserve team boss Mike Walker, an appointment that was treated with some local cynicism at the time, but it turned out to be an inspired one! Neal went on to coach England alongside Graham Taylor; he assisted Taylor as they failed to qualify for the 1994 World Cup finals.

DRAW KINGS

NORWICH drew 23 out of their 42 Division One fixtures in the 1978/79 season, a record for the top division which still stands. Only the three relegated clubs won fewer games.

THE BARRY BUTLER TROPHY

VERSUS ARSENAL

AS Arsenal have constantly played in the top division of English football since 1920, it was not until September 1972 that the teams met for the first time in a competitive league match, Norwich winning 3-2 at Carrow Road with Terry Anderson (twice) and David Cross scoring. Their first-ever meeting had come 20 years earlier, Arsenal winning 5-0 in an FA Cup third-round tie at Carrow Road. Future Norwich loanee John Hartson scored a hat-trick as the Gunners won 5-1 in April 1995, and, in Norwich's last Premiership season to date, the Canaries lost 4-1, home and away, Thierry Henry scoring a hat-trick in the Highbury fixture on April 2nd 2005. Norwich had perhaps their most famous win on the opening day of the inaugural Premiership season. 2-0 down at half-time, Norwich rallied to win 4-2. The four second-half goals coming in fifteen minutes were scored by Mark Robins (twice), David Phillips and Ruel Fox. Norwich have not beaten the Gunners in the nine meetings between the clubs since then. In total, the clubs have played 49 competitive league and cup games, Norwich winning 10, Arsenal 22, with 17 being drawn.

HOLT THE CHEF

ONE of the more familiar soundbites surrounding televised Norwich matches in recent years was the reference to midfielder Gary Holt as an 'ex-Army chef'. This was despite his time spent in the military having elapsed nearly ten years before he had joined Norwich. However, this little fact was food and drink in itself for headline writers, who could not help mixing Holt's culinary past with the fact that Delia Smith was Norwich's majority shareholder! Bought from Kilmarnock for £135,000 in 2001, Holt – whose energetic style earnt him the nickname 'Three Lungs' – made 168 league appearances for Norwich scoring three goals.

OH DEANO!

WITH a scoring record of 56 goals in 211 appearances for Fulham – his first club – big things were expected of Dean Coney when Norwich signed him from QPR for £350,000 in 1989. He made just 17 appearances, scoring one goal, the opener in a 2-2 draw against Aston Villa at Carrow Road on April 22nd 1989.

COLLAPSE

WITH a half-time score of 0-0 in their home Division Three (South) game against Southend United on November 2nd 1946, few Norwich fans were prepared for the side's sudden collapse in the second half, as Southend rattled in five goals, the sole Norwich consolation coming from Bernard Robinson. The Canaries clearly had a porous defence at the time, as, at the end of the season, they had conceded exactly 100 league goals, 12 of those coming in two consecutive league games at Christmas. They played three league games in four days over that period, losing 1-0 at Bournemouth on Christmas Day, before being turned over 6-1 by the same side on Boxing Day, then, two days after that losing 6-1, again, this time at Cardiff City. And to think today's clubs complain of fixture congestion!

FINAL DRESS REHEARSAL

THE season before the two clubs met at Wembley in the 1985 League Cup Final, Norwich and Sunderland met in the third round of the same competition, in January 1984. After a 0-0 draw in front of just 12,406 spectators at Carrow Road, Norwich won the replay at Roker Park 2-1.

FOUR-GAME TIE

IT took Norwich four games to dispose of Birmingham City in the FA Cup third round the following season! A 0-0 draw at St Andrew's on January 5th 1985 was followed, on January 23rd, by a 1-1 draw at Norwich. The teams went back to Birmingham three days later for another 1-1 draw, before Norwich finally prevailed, two days on, winning a third replay 1-0 at Carrow Road, Steve Bruce scoring the goal. One week later, Norwich were out of the competition, losing 2-1 at West Ham United, Louie Donowa scoring.

UNLUCKY ALAN!

ALAN Bullimore, a left-half who joined Norwich as a schoolboy in October 1953, waited for nearly three and a half years until he made his Canaries debut, a Division Three (South) game against Torquay on 23rd February 1957. Norwich lost, 7-1, and Bullimore never played for the club again, seeing out his career with non-league Gorleston.

KEN'S SELECTION CHANGE

COMMENTING on the Canaries' two-legged League Cup semi-final success over Ipswich Town in 1985, Norwich manager Ken Brown admitted to a sense of relief that the side had turned the match around in that second leg, saying that he thought he might have made a selection error in the game's first leg, which Norwich lost 1-0. Brown would not clarify what that error was, but he did make two changes to the Norwich side for that second leg, John Devine missing out for Paul Haylock and young forward Paul Clayton also being replaced with Louie Donowa. Did Brown think that Clayton's lack of experience (that first-leg tie had been his first appearance of the season and only his fourth in total for the club) had weakened the team's attacking edge in that game, or did his decision to select John Devine at right-back, by then a player established in midfield, weaken the Canaries defence? Only Brown knows the answer and it may be one of those possibilities, both – or neither. As things turned out, Donowa kept his place for the final, whilst Devine made the final squad, as a non-playing substitute.

PAUL CLAYTON

PAUL was an important member of the Canaries 1983 FA Youth Cup-winning side who scored eight goals in the side's successful run, including two in the final against Everton. However, he was unable to reproduce his obvious potential in the first team, and, after making fifteen appearances in five years, moved to Darlington for what was, at the time, a record transfer fee for the Quakers of £25,000.

HIGHEST AND LOWEST

THE Canaries' highest league position was third in the inaugural Premiership season of 1992/93. Despite this and ultimately just missing out on winning English football's greatest prize, Norwich ended the season on a negative goal difference of minus four! The club's lowest-ever finishing position was bottom of the old Division Three (South) in 1930/31 and 1956/57. Interestingly, in that 1956/57 season, Norwich scored as many goals (61) as they did when finishing third in that opening Premiership season. They also conceded 94 goals, giving a goal difference of minus 33!

IS VIC THERE?

THE honour of scoring Norwich's first-ever league goal goes to one Victor Whitham, who scored in the 1-1 draw at Plymouth Argyle in the club's opening Division Three game on August 28th 1920.

JUST WILLIAM

THE following season saw the lower leagues split into Division 3 (South) and (North). Thus, on August 29th 1921, the splendidly named William Bertram scored Norwich's first goal in the rebranded Division 3 (South) game in a 1-1 draw, again, at Plymouth Argyle.

BONE GOAL

FAST forward to August 12th 1972 and Jim Bone books his place in the history books, as he was the scorer of Norwich's first-ever goal in Division One, his second half opportunist strike securing a 1-1 draw in the Carrow Road clash against Everton. The first win followed three days later, a 2-1 success at rivals Ipswich Town, Bone and Terry Anderson scoring.

COCK ROBINS

MARK Robins scored the first Norwich City goal in the Premiership. Debuting as a second-half substitute against Arsenal at Highbury on August 15th 1992, he scored the first of his two goals in Norwich's 4-2 victory, in the 69th minute. Norwich fans can therefore always claim that their team was the first to beat Arsenal, home or away, in the Premiership!

WINNING LINE-UP

THE side that beat Arsenal in that memorable first Premiership match for the Canaries (if not for Arsenal!) was Gunn: Culverhouse, Bowen, Butterworth, Polston, Megson (Crook, 87); Fox, Newman, Sutton (Robins, 58), Goss and Phillips. That same game also saw midfielder Jeremy Goss become the first Norwich player to get a yellow card in their Premiership history.

NORWICH CITY MANAGERS

Since 1905, Norwich City have had a total of 35 managers. Significant names/appointments include:

First Manager – John Bowman......................................1905-1907
Longest Serving – Ken Brown.......................................1980-1987
Shortest Serving – Martin O'Neill........August to December 1995
Highest Win Ratio – 50% – Norman Low (129 in 258 games)
....1950-1955
Lowest Win Ratio – 26.5% – Albert Gosnall (59 in 223 games)
....1921-1926
Most Games – 367 – Ken Brown 1980-1987
Fewest Games – 20 – George Swindin 1962

GEORGE Swindin also had a win percentage of 50%. However, I have prioritised Low's impressive record as it was over 258 games, not 20, as was the case with Swindin. Cyril Spiers had a lower win ratio of just 23.1%. This has been discounted as he did not have at least one full season in charge of the Canaries. As for George Swindin, he swiftly left the club to manage Cardiff City, as Spiers did after just 65 games in 1947.

CHRISTMAS FEAST

AS was the tradition at the time, clubs were expected to play two games over two days at Christmas from the 1920s to 1940s, with games frequently played on Christmas Day and Boxing Day. These fixtures invariably produced goals in abundance, although the intelligence of the fixture compilers does need to be questioned with regard to some of the scheduling. For example, over Christmas in 1935 the Canaries were scheduled to play Bury, home and away, a 400-mile plus return trip for each side – nonsensical considering Norwich could have played any one of four London teams at that time, or Leicester City, a return trip of a little over 200 miles. Needless to say, the exhausting Boxing Day trip to Norwich for that fixture must have taken its toll on that Bury side, for, after their 1-0 win over the Canaries at Christmas, they succumbed to a 5-3 defeat in the follow up fixture the next day. The Norwich scorers were Jack Vinall (2), John Friar (2), and Cecil Russell.

FINEST SEASON?

MANY speak of Norwich's finish of third in the Premiership's 1992/93 season as the finest campaign in the club's history. But it could be argued that Dave Stringer's team in 1988/89 was at least its equal. The Canaries finished fourth in the First Division at the end of that campaign, a mere two points behind Nottingham Forest in third. The team won eight of their first 11 games that season, as well as beating Port Vale, Sutton United, Sheffield United and West Ham United to make their first FA Cup semi-final since 1959, where they lost, 1-0, to Everton. Stringer's side won plaudits for its attractive, passing game and featured players such as Andy Townsend, Dale Gordon and Mark Bowen. Highlights included a league double over Manchester United and five successive away wins at the start of the season. The side did not drop out of the top two places in the division from September through till the following March (they were top for two months, from October to Christmas) dramatically, as is the Norwich way, running out of steam towards the end, winning only two of their last ten league games, including a televised 5-0 defeat at Arsenal, future Norwich loanee David Rocastle scoring two. Unlike their third-place Premiership season in 1993, however, Norwich did manage to finish this one with a positive goal difference, albeit of only plus three!

LONG LIVE THE KING!

ON October 29th 1938, King George VI became the first reigning monarch to attend a league match in England when he visited the ground for the game against Millwall. Unfortunately, Norwich did not put on a performance for their regal visitor and lost 2-0. It seems that the King was not much of a football fan anyway, as he departed proceedings with barely a quarter of an hour played!

KING AND CAPTAIN

THE captain of Norwich City at the time of the King's brief visit was Tom Smalley who was at Norwich for only that 1938/39 season. Smalley arrived from Wolves that summer for a fee of £4,500, playing in 43 games, scoring one goal (against Swansea) before moving on to Northampton Town after the war, and making over 200 appearances for the Cobblers.

TV ANDY

ITV Football co-commentator Andy Townsend has Norwich City to thank for raising his profile in the game and setting him out on the career he ultimately had with Chelsea, Aston Villa and Middlesbrough, as well as two World Cups with the Republic of Ireland. Townsend was in and out of the Southampton side when Norwich paid £300,000 for him in August 1988. He made 36 league appearances in that season for Norwich, scoring five goals, as well as two in the club's run to the FA Cup semi-final, both against Port Vale in the third round, one of them being a superb long distance chip. The 1989/90 season was less successful for Norwich (less successful at the time meant 'only' finishing tenth in the First Division!) and, at the end of a campaign that saw him make a further 44 appearances, scoring three goals, Townsend went to the 1990 World Cup in Italy with a move on his mind. Sure enough, it came that August, when Chelsea paid £1.2 million to take him to Stamford Bridge. He had played in all five of the Republic of Ireland's World Cup matches that summer, including their quarter-final defeat to Italy, becoming the first, and, thus far, only player to have appeared in a World Cup quarter-final whilst playing for Norwich City.

RADIO IWAN

NORWICH City legend Iwan Roberts has also settled into a media career following his retirement from the game and is regularly seen or heard on both Sky Sports and BBC Radio Cymru doing a Welsh language co-commentary on Wales internationals.

THE ASSISTANTS

DURING the 2009/10 season, both Manchester's United and City had ex-Norwich players as their assistant managers. Mike Phelan was number two to Sir Alex Ferguson at Old Trafford, whilst Mark Bowen held the same position at Eastlands under Mark Hughes before Hughes' dismissal. In addition, Kevin Bond, who played at both Norwich and Manchester City under his father, John, was assistant to Harry Redknapp at Tottenham Hotspur. The Premiership of that season also had three ex-Norwich players as club managers; Martin O'Neill at Aston Villa, Steve Bruce at Sunderland, and, up until December 2009, Gary Megson at Bolton Wanderers.

CARROW ROAD

NORWICH moved into their current home in 1935, the original ground taking just 82 days to build! The all-time record attendance of 43,984, for an FA Cup quarter-final tie against Leicester City in 1963, is unlikely to ever be surpassed, certainly in the short term, so 'modern' records are measured against its status as an all-seater stadium. That record is 25,522 for the Premiership match against Manchester United in April 2005, which Norwich won 2-0. The present Carrow Road has four stands, the Barclay and Norwich & Peterborough stands, which are behind each goal, plus the two main stands, the Geoffrey Watling City Stand, and, most recently, the Jarrold Stand, which was opened in 2004. The 2009/10 ground capacity was 26,018, broken down as follows: Jarrold Stand (including Aviva Community Stand), 9,892; the Barclay Stand, 6,107; the Norwich & Peterborough Stand, 5,799; and the City Stand, 4,173. The remaining areas of the stadium allowing for another 47 persons. Prior to the start of the 2010/11 season, the club announced plans to install 1,000 new seats throughout the ground, taking the capacity up to 27,000. The 'new' City stand replaced the previous structure that was destroyed by fire in 1984. A popular story of the time surrounded Norwich striker John Deehan who was said to have turned up for training on the day following the fire dressed as a fireman. The ground is the most easterly stadium in the UK, and, as is the fashion for Norfolk, has its own quirk with the South (now Jarrold) stand being sited on its easterly side! The traditional 'singing' stand at Carrow Road is the Barclay, one which, in the days before all-seater stadiums was always full, noisy, and extremely boisterous – not for the faint hearted! Justin Fashanu's famous turn and volley for Norwich against Liverpool in 1980 was scored in front of the Barclay end, as was Jerry Goss's equaliser for the Canaries against Bayern Munich in 1993. The Barclay is the most traditionally supporter-orientated stand at the club and remains as lively as ever, even with all seating now being the norm and, with its very own 'son of the Barclay' now in place (the infill between the City Stand and the Barclay), known officially as the 'Thorpe Corner', but, at the club as 'The Snakepit'. It will, no doubt, remain the focus of singing and chanting at Carrow Road for many years to come – including, no doubt, the familiar calls to 'sing up the South Stand', where the residents can be a little more vocally reserved at times!

BC (BEFORE CARROW ROAD)

PRIOR to construction on the Jarrold stand, the Norfolk Archaeological Unit (NAU) excavated the site in 2003. Their findings led them to conclude that the ground was standing on the site of an ancient hunting camp, originating as far back as 11,500BC. Amongst their finds were distinctive long flint hunting blades, and further finds of 'bruised' blades, used for sharpening other implements. The camp would have been one of many in River Wensum valley at the time in what would have been a cold landscape, populated by herds of reindeer and wild horses. 'Wild horses' may well have dragged early man to what was eventually Carrow Road at that time! A unique feature of Carrow Road would be that it is the only football ground sited above another form of meeting place, that, over 10,000 years previously, would also have hosted numerous folk whose passion would have been hunting reindeer in what were near-Arctic conditions. Perhaps they used the orange ball – or rather, spears?

GOING LOCO

WHEN the London & North Eastern Railway built their new range of class B17/4 locomotives in the 1930s, those that were for use on the East Coast mainline were named after a selection of football clubs, of which, 'The Norwich City' was one. When these steam locomotives were scrapped 30 or so years later, there was great demand for their nameplates, the 'Norwich City' plate ultimately ending up at Carrow Road where it is now installed, permanently, just inside the players' tunnel. Who needs 'This Is Anfield'?

RYAN'S EXPRESS

SIGNED for £40,000 from Luton Town in 1976, full-back John Ryan played 40 of the 45 games during that 1976/77 season, coming off the bench and scoring in the Canaries' 2-2 draw at Manchester United following an early spell out through injury. He made a goalscoring impact the following season: as an ever-present, he scored 15 times in 42 league appearances, including goals in four consecutive games against Ipswich Town, Coventry City, Middlesbrough and West Ham United, eventually ending the season as leading league goalscorer, three ahead of Kevin Reeves, whose own goalscoring prowess would lead to a £1 million move to Manchester City.

THE OLD FARM

NORWICH City and Ipswich Town have played each other in a total of 91 competitive league and cup matches; Norwich winning 35 games and Ipswich 40, with only 16 draws – less than 18% of all fixtures played, a very low figure, especially for 'derby' games, that tend to be tight. The clubs had originally met in the Norfolk & Suffolk League, playing six times between 1902 and 1905 (one of only two league defeats Norwich had in their title-winning season of 1904/05 was the final game of that season, at Ipswich) before Norwich's elevation to the Southern League the following season meant that the two did not renew their rivalry until the first Division Three (South) campaign following World War II, Ipswich winning that fixture on September 7th 1946 by 5-0. The game was goalkeeper Fred Hall's 94th and final for Norwich. Ipswich duly won the return fixture at Carrow Road, 1-0, the following January, and, in terms of games won, Norwich have mostly been playing catch-up ever since! It didn't get much better for Norwich the following season either, the fixture on September 13th 1947 saw the Blues rattle in five goals again, <u>and</u> at Carrow Road, the sole response, and the first scored by a Norwich player against Ipswich, coming from John Church. Interestingly, the Norwich goalkeeper on that day, Derek Davis, did live to be picked again, unlike the unfortunate Hall, but only on another two occasions before his Norwich career also came to an end. Norwich's first league success came in January 1948 with a 2-1 win, Bernard Robinson and Allenby Driver the scorers. Norwich finished a distant 20th in the Division Three (South) that season, Ipswich finishing a not-so-distant 15 points ahead, albeit in fourth place. The clubs first met in cup competition in a FA Cup fourth-round tie in January 1962, drawing 1-1 at Carrow Road, before Norwich won the replay, 2-1, at Portman Road, Terry Allcock scoring both goals; he had also been the Norwich goalscorer in the original tie. This was quite a shock, as Ipswich went on to win the First Division championship that same season, Norwich finishing a lowly 17th in Division Two. The clubs met in the League Cup for the first time six years later, Norwich triumphing 4-2 at Carrow Road, Hugh Curran scoring a hat-trick. It was another disappointing league campaign for the Canaries, who ended that 1968/69 season in 13th position, whilst Ipswich finished, a division higher, in 12th.

THE pair had a much more famous League Cup encounter in 1985, where, over the two-legged semi-final, Norwich won 2-1 on aggregate, Steve Bruce scoring a late winner at Carrow Road that took Norwich to Wembley and a date with Sunderland. Hostilities between the two teams in the top division, meanwhile, had eventually commenced in 1972/73, the first-ever First Division (ultimately Premiership) fixture between the clubs taking place in only the second game of that season, Norwich following up their opening-day 1-1 draw against Everton with an impressive 2-1 win at Portman Road on August 15th, goals by Jimmy Bone and Terry Anderson upsetting the very great majority of a Portman Road crowd that was approaching 30,000. That win took Norwich to fifth place in the First Division table, and was one of only four home defeats Ipswich suffered that season, as they ended the season in fourth spot, Norwich surviving relegation by just two points. That early away victory made all the difference at the end of that season! The return fixture was a 0-0 draw at Carrow Road on November 11th, in front of 34,640. Remarkably, although that game was already Norwich's 17th league fixture that season, manager Ron Saunders' team selection that day saw eight players feature, all of whom had started the previous 16 games. The players were Kevin Keelan, Duncan Forbes, Max Briggs, Doug Livermore, Jimmy Bone, David Cross, Graham Paddon and Terry Anderson. Following that 0-0 draw Norwich were eighth in the First Division, unbeaten at home, and only below Ipswich on goal difference. It looked, therefore, as if the two sides were all set to have a top-flight rivalry for many seasons to come. However, that was not to be the case; Norwich finished the following season, 1973/74, bottom and were relegated, losing the home Boxing Day fixture 2-1 in front of another large crowd, 29,637. Ted MacDougall scored the first of his 66 league and cup goals for Norwich on that day. The clubs' first fixture in the Premiership was on December 21st 1992, Ipswich triumphing 2-1 at Carrow Road in what was Norwich's first home defeat that season. Ipswich went on to win the return fixture at Portman Road 3-1 the following April, thus completing the double over that Norwich team that eventually finished third, their best-ever finish. Had Norwich just won and drawn those two games, Ipswich would have been relegated, and the Canaries would have finished second, which, somehow, takes some of the gloss off that remarkable season!

PICKED AND GONE

MICHAEL Pickering joined Norwich on loan from Sheffield Wednesday in September 1983, but only played for a total of 16 minutes whilst at the club, those coming as a substitute in the 3-3 draw against Manchester United on October 1st. The man he replaced that day, Dave Watson, had a rather more illustrious career with Norwich, missing just two league games that season and making a total of 256 appearances for the club.

DRAW THAT FELT LIKE A WIN

IN that Carrow Road clash against United, Norwich had gone 3-0 down, only to rescue the game with three second-half goals from Dave Bennett, Mike Channon and Louie Donowa. It was Donowa's first league start for the Canaries, he went on to start another 22 league games that season, ending it with four league goals, including the opener in a 2-0 win at Everton.

LOUIE LOUIE

ALTHOUGH born in Ipswich, Louie Donowa swiftly became a crowd favourite at Norwich, the winger's explosive pace and unpredictability causing problems for opposition defences, and, sometimes, his own teammates! He made a total of 80 appearances for Norwich, scoring 15 goals, before an impressive spell in Spain at Deportivo La Coruna where he made 85 appearances, scoring 20 goals. He had a short spell at Ipswich in 1989/90 before moving on again, including a spell in Finland at Turun Palloseura.

FINLAND, FINLAND, FINLAND

ALTHOUGH no player from Finland has played for Norwich, the club did have Bolton Wanderers and Finland international goalkeeper Jussi Jaaskelainen on trial in 1997. He played for Norwich reserves in a 1-0 victory over Luton Town, before returning to Finland, Mike Walker prevaricating whether to sign him or not. Bolton Wanderers stepped in and did, for £100,000 – although it probably ensured Robert Green's consequent fine career at Norwich. Third-choice Canaries keeper at the time Green, the second Norwich goalkeeper to play for England, would almost certainly have moved on. Jaasskelainen has since made over 400 appearances for Bolton.

THE SAINTS

NORWICH'S first home fixture upon their elevation to the Southern League in 1905 was against Southampton at Newmarket Road on September 9th. They could not mark the occasion with a win, the game ending as a 0-0 draw.

THE 39 CANARIES

NORWICH used 39 different players in the 1908/09 season, 11 of whom only made two or less appearances. Records then, however, were not always accurate, and the club's playing statistics for that season show that 'A. Canary' made three appearances!

VIVA ESPANA!

SPAIN under-21 midfielder Victor Segura joined Norwich on a free transfer from UE Lleida in 1997. Segura was expected to provide a much needed creative spark to the Norwich midfield under Mike Walker's second spell. The move never worked out and he was released in 1999 after just 33 games.

BIG RON

HOLYWELL-born Ron Davies is best known for his scoring exploits for Southampton, a haul of 134 goals in 240 league games for the Saints and the assertion from Sir Matt Busby that he was "the greatest centre-forward in Europe". Before joining Southampton in 1966, Davies spent three seasons at Norwich, scoring 66 goals in 126 appearances. Following his arrival from Luton Town in September 1963, Davies scored in his first four league games, ending that first season on 30 senior goals, a distant 17 ahead of his closest teammate, Tommy Bryceland. The following two seasons saw a further 36 goals scored as Davies became a huge favourite at Carrow Road. However, despite his scoring exploits, Norwich continued to scratch around mid-table, and Southampton signed him for £55,000, a fee Norwich fans considered derisory and for which manager Lol Morgan received a lot of criticism. The eventual signing of Hugh Curran tempered the loss somewhat, but Davies's contribution to City is not forgotten; he remains in the top-ten goalscorers, and became an inaugural member of the club's 'Hall of Fame' in 2003.

ON TRIAL!

THE need for financial caution during Bruce Rioch's managerial reign at Carrow Road saw 17 players arrive at Colney for a 'trial' in the 1999/2000 season, none of whom were deigned good enough by the manager to sign permanently. This led to some criticism at the time, with supporters claiming the revolving door policy was designed to look as if the club was actively looking to secure new singings, without actually having to do so. However, Rioch's conclusions on those players' abilities has been proved to be extremely sound, as none of the 17 in question have gone on to significantly make a name for themselves in the game, the best known perhaps being left-back Hasney Aljofree who has had a decent career at Dundee United, Plymouth Argyle and Swindon Town.

IN IT FOR THE MARNEY

THAT game against Plymouth Argyle was one of the 15 appearances midfielder Dean Marney made for Norwich in a loan spell from Tottenham Hotspur. After suffering an injury whilst at the club, Marney returned to Tottenham for treatment. Upon his return to fitness, despite rumours of his return, Norwich declared no interest in bringing him back, either on loan or permanently. Marney joined Hull City in 2006 and became an integral figure in their promotion to – and first two seasons spent in – the Premiership.

THE TOTTENHAM CONNECTION

MARNEY is just one of 29 players to have played for both Norwich City and Tottenham Hotspur. Six prominent names on that list are players who have come to Norwich from White Hart Lane, initially as relative unknowns, but all names that went on to become vital members of their respective Norwich teams. They include; Mark Bowen, Ian Crook, Ian Culverhouse, Gary Doherty, Paul McVeigh and John Polston. A slightly more famous name was Martin Peters. Ex-England international Martin Chivers had a spell at Norwich, following his return from Switzerland in 1978, scoring on his debut against Southampton, whilst two Norwich players who have gone on to feature prominently for Tottenham are Ruel Fox and Tim Sherwood, although both joined via other clubs, namely Newcastle United and Blackburn Rovers.

OOR WULLIE

THE signing of Scottish international full-back Willie Donachie from Manchester City for £200,000 in September 1981 was regarded as quite a coup for manager Ken Brown. However, despite his name, reputation, and the fee, Donachie found it difficult to shift established defender Greg Downs. He displaced Downs for 11 games, but, after Downs regained his place in the side for the Carrow Road clash against Luton Town on December 28th, Donachie never appeared for the club again. Downs missed just one more match that campaign and went on to win the Barry Butler trophy for Player of the Year. Donachie, meanwhile, got Norwich their money back when he left for Portland Timbers in the USA in March 1982.

WALKER OUT

MIKE Walker's return to Norwich as manager in June 1996 saw many Norwich fans dreaming of a swift return to the glorious spell of football they had enjoyed under his initial period in charge. However, the team's Premiership days were just a memory by then, and they and Walker struggled to make an impact in the First Division. With further relegation a distinct possibility in 1998, Walker eased those fears by guiding the club to two consecutive 5-0 victories in the last two home games against Huddersfield Town and Swindon Town. In a season where the team's highest league placing had been 10th, it was too little, too late, and he was sacked five days after the Swindon victory.

THE OWL ATTRACTION

SHEFFIELD Wednesday have the distinction of being one of the top crowd pullers at each of the three grounds Norwich have played at. The crowd of 10,366 who saw their FA Cup first-round game against the Canaries in January 1908 was the second-highest ever at Newmarket Road, whilst the attendance of 25,057 in the fifth-round tie in February 1935 was the highest ever at The Nest. Finally, when the two clubs met, again in the FA Cup, again in the fifth round, on March 11th 1967, 41,000 packed into Carrow Road, making it the fourth highest attendance ever at the current crowd. Interestingly, but perhaps not untypically, just one week later, only 13,015 turned up for the home Division Two clash against Blackburn Rovers.

HOOPS FOILED

QUEENS Park Rangers travelled to Carrow Road for a First Division meeting with Norwich on April 17th 1976, top of the table, one point ahead of Liverpool, with both having three games to play. Under the management of Dave Sexton, QPR had made themselves favourites for the championship as the season drew to an end, and victory was expected at Carrow Road to further back those claims. However, in front of a crowd of 30,895, their biggest of the season, Norwich beat the odds with a 3-2 win, Peter Morris, Ted MacDougall and Phil Boyer scoring the goals. Rangers ended the season in second place, one point behind eventual champions Liverpool. Interestingly, had QPR held onto the half-time score of 1-1, their end of season record would have been absolutely identical to Liverpool's, and the Football League would have needed a play-off match to decide that season's champions. A final score of 0-0, however, would have seen QPR win the title by 0.03 of a goal! Luckily, this was the last season that teams level on points had their final positions determined by the complexities of goal average, the far easier system of goal difference being introduced for the 1976/77 season.

MORRIS MAJOR

IN scoring Norwich's opening goal in the above game, Peter Morris could be said to be the man who ended QPR's title challenge that season. It was the only goal he scored in his Norwich career, spanning 86 league and cup appearances, following his £60,000 arrival from Ipswich Town in June 1974.

NIGHTINGALE AMONGST CANARIES

MARK Nightingale was a first-team squad member for Norwich from 1977 until 1981, and a player of whom big things were expected when he signed from Crystal Palace. Despite his progress being marked by his regular involvement with the England youth side, the Salisbury-born midfielder never became a first-team regular at City, settling back at his first club, AFC Bournemouth, after a brief spell playing in Hong Kong. His Norwich record during that four-year period was just 32 league and cup appearances, including seven as a substitute; his debut coming from the bench in the 2-1 Division One victory over Wolves in October 1977.

FIRST SUBSTITUTE

GORDON Bolland was the first Norwich substitute, coming on for Terry Anderson in the Canaries' 0-0 draw at Bristol City on August 31st 1965. Norwich made use of that new rule just five times in the whole of the 1965/66 season. The first Norwich player to come on in a game and score a goal was Trevor Howard, whose cameo appearance in the clash against Hull City earned Norwich their 1-0 victory. Sadly for Howard, his historical effort gave him no reward, and he didn't appear for the team again until the end of the following March when, again, he was substitute, this time coming on for Bryan Conlon at Sheffield United.

HOWARD'S WAY

TREVOR Howard was never quite the leading man at Norwich that his famous acting namesake was. In all, he appeared as a substitute for the club 45 times, as well as being the unused 12th man on a further 20 occasions.

JACK OF CLUB

ANOTHER Canary with proven bench experience was Scottish forward Ross Jack, who, of his 67 appearances (14 goals) for the club from 1980 to 1983, came on as a substitute in 28 of them! Fittingly, his last appearance for Norwich, against West Bromwich Albion on May 2nd 1983, was also as a number 12, replacing Dave Watson as City, 1-0 down, searched in vain for an equaliser. Jack started his Norwich career wearing the number five shirt and was substituted himself in only his second league start for the club, being replaced by Joe Royle in the Canaries' 6-1 dismembering at Middlesbrough on October 4th 1980.

SUB SIXTEEN

THE players who made way for Ross Jack in his stint of 28 substitute appearances for Norwich are as follows: Mark Barham (4); Keith Bertschin (4); Paul Haylock (3); Peter Mendham (3); John Deehan (2); Mick McGuire (2); Dave Bennett (1); Mike Channon (1); Greg Downs (1); Steve Goble (1); Aage Hareide (1); John McDowell (1); Drazen Muzinic (1); Mark Nightingale (1); Denis Van Wijk (1); and Dave Watson (1).

BIG SQUAD

NORWICH used 29 different players during their 42-game Division One campaign of 1979/80, of which nine squad members made six appearances or less. Doug Evans, Greig Shepherd and Phil Lythgoe all appeared just once in the league, Lythgoe as a substitute in the 2-0 Carrow Road win over Bristol City on December 15th, his last appearance for the club.

FATHER AND SON

DERRICK and Phil Lythgoe both played for Norwich City. Derrick's career at the club, from 1958 to 1962, encompassed 74 appearances and 29 goals. Following his retirement, Lythgoe senior settled in the area, Norwich-born son Phil joining the club in 1977, following a trial at Bolton Wanderers, the club of his father's birthplace. Lythgoe junior was not as successful for City as his father, making a total of just 12 appearances, his sole goal coming in the 3-1 home defeat to Manchester United on April 15th 1978.

DADDY'S BOY

BOTH John Bond and his successor as Norwich manager, Ken Brown, had sons who played for the club under their stewardship. Centre-back Kevin Bond, who made 161 appearances for the Canaries, was a defender who has the other distinction of scoring a goal and an own goal in the same match. Quite an achievement, except that he did it on two consecutive occasions in March 1980! Kenny Brown, also a defender, made 25 appearances for the club from 1985 to 1988.

THE CARETAKER

IN the brief period from the summers of 1998 till 2009, Norwich have had, up to present incumbent Paul Lambert, a total of 11 first-team managers. Four of those were 'caretaker' managers, with neither one of John Faulkner (1998), Martin Hunter (2006), Jim Duffy (2007) nor Ian Butterworth (2009) staying at the club following the appointment of their respective successors. Of the six games they managed between them, only Faulkner secured a victory, that being a 1-0 success at Reading on the last day of the 1997/98 season.

TEXACO TRIALS

FROM 1972 to 1975, the Canaries took part in the Texaco Cup, a knockout competition featuring English and Scottish clubs that hadn't qualified for Europe. Norwich's first foray into the competition was their reward for winning the Division Two championship in the 1971/72 season. They duly met Dundee in the first round in September 1972, losing 2-1 (Bone) in the first leg at Dens Park, a game that saw goalkeeper Mervyn Cawston, (who had the unenviable task of being cover for Kevin Keelan) make his first and only appearance for the club that season, alongside centre-back Andy Rollings who was also cover, for defensive mainstay Duncan Forbes. Both Keelan and Forbes were back for the second leg, on September 27th 1972, where City won 2-0, another Jimmy Bone strike and an own goal seeing them through on aggregate. Leicester City followed in the second round, and, in front of an impressive home crowd of 18,513, Norwich won 2-0, levelling the scores over the two games to 2-2, and winning on penalties after extra time – the first time Norwich had been involved in a penalty shoot-out in a competitive match. The club therefore found itself in a second cup semi-final that season; they had turfed Chelsea out of the League Cup at that stage back in December and they now found Motherwell standing in between them and another chance of cup glory. The first leg was played at Carrow Road on March 14th 1973, a little over a week since Norwich's Wembley disappointment against Tottenham, Ron Saunders selecting six of that game's starting eleven, the Canaries prevailing 2-0, both goals coming from winger Ian Mellor. An exciting second leg at Motherwell followed, but, City were, by now, hardened cup fighters, the game being their sixteenth cup match that season, with Mellor and another own goal contributing to a 3-2 defeat that, nevertheless, saw them win 4-3 on aggregate. Fittingly, the final was an all East Anglian affair, with Ipswich Town the opponents, the Blues winning the first leg at Portman Road 2-1, repeating that scoreline and lifting the trophy, 4-2 on aggregate, at Carrow Road on May 7th, over a week since the league season had finished. The attendance for that game, 35,798, was the club's second highest all season, and bettered that of their first-ever Division One game, back in August, by just under 10,000. Texaco Cup fever clearly had arrived in Norfolk, thus ensuring the club would enter the competition for a further two seasons.

MISSED BALL

WORLD Cup winner Alan Ball was thought to be very close to signing for the Canaries when he left Arsenal in 1976, a £50,000 transfer having been agreed between the two clubs. However, Ball chose to join Southampton, thus denying manager John Bond and the club's fans the opportunity of seeing Ball and Martin Peters playing in the same midfield.

FOG STOPS PLAY

LEADING 3-2, and 5-2 up on aggregate, Norwich were five minutes from Wembley in the second leg of their 1973 League Cup semi-final against Chelsea when thick fog descended on the ground making visibility so poor that referee Gordon Hill abandoned the game. Chelsea did not capitalise on their great escape and, when the game was replayed on January 3rd 1973, the Canaries won 1-0, Steve Govier, who replaced skipper Duncan Forbes, scoring the goal.

HANNAH TIME

DEFENDER Joe Hannah decided that one of his poorer displays for Norwich merited self punishment, 'sentencing' himself to walk home from the club after that game, the not so gentle stroll to Sheringham being a 25-mile walk! The conscientious Hannah was a one-club man, playing for Norwich from 1921 through to 1935, making 427 appearances.

WORLD-RECORD TRANSFER

WHEN Wolves' Bryn Jones signed for Arsenal in 1938, the fee of £14,000 was the highest ever paid at the time, and even led to questions about the ethics of the move being raised in Parliament! He signed for Norwich in 1949, going on to make 26 league appearances.

KEANE ARRIVES

ROBBIE Keane first announced his footballing (and gymnastic) prowess on August 9th 1997, scoring both goals in his professional debut as Wolves beat Norwich 2-0 at Carrow Road.

UPS AND DOWNS

ALL seemed well at Norwich after the 3-1 home win over Ipswich Town on October 11th 1996, the team sat at the top of Division One, having only lost one of their preceding ten games. However, the Canaries only won two of their following 13 fixtures, including consecutive thrashings at West Bromwich Albion and Port Vale by 5-1 and 6-1 respectively, the latter game seeing them slump to 10th in the league. The 6-1 debacle at Port Vale led to Mike Walker making the astute signing of Matt Jackson, the talented central defender joining from Everton for £450,000. It didn't end there; Jackson's debut at Queens Park Rangers saw Norwich lose again, 3-2, Bryan Gunn now having seen 14 goals go past him in just three games. Jackson's arrival did signify a City renaissance; the club won their next four games to creep back into fourth place, City fans now daring to dream of a play-off place again. That was pretty much it for the 1996/97 season, the one which had seen Walker's return to the club. An impressive 2-1 win at Stoke City had put Norwich into that fourth place, but, following that game, the club only won three of its last 18 fixtures, the final game of the season seeing a miserable 3-0 capitulation at relegated Oldham Athletic, ex-Canary Matthew Rush scoring one of the goals.

TAKE TWO

DESPITE that second half of the season collapse in 1997, Norwich went into the 1997/98 campaign with confidence, Walker's gradually reshaped squad demonstrating that they would be a force to contend with that season by losing all of their first three league fixtures. The entire season was a disappointing one, Norwich briefly got as high tenth in the league (following a typically feisty 2-1 home win over Ipswich Town on September 26th) but flattered to deceive for most of it, winning only 14 of their 46 league matches, their final goals tally of 52 being somewhat flattered by two consecutive 5-0 home victories (over Huddersfield Town and Swindon Town) in April. Mike Walker had returned to the club charged with the specific goal of getting them back to the Premiership, but, after those two extremely average seasons with him at the helm, Walker resigned just before the last game of the season which Norwich duly – typically – won, 1-0 at Reading.

MIKE WALKER

BOGEY SIDE?

WHENEVER Norwich are due to play Crystal Palace, the united cry on internet messageboards, the local media, and at the ground is that Palace are the Canaries' 'bogey' side, one who the club never plays well – or gets a good result – against. Looking back at the fixtures between the two clubs there is more evidence to suggest that they are both pretty much level pegging with each other, results-wise. The two have met in 46 competitive league matches (League Divisions One, Two, the Premiership and the Championship) since Norwich's promotion to the First Division in 1972, and, of those games, Norwich have won 18 times and Palace 17, with 11 draws. So Norwich, despite the claims, have the slight ascendancy. When that game period is cut in half, things are different. The last 23 competitive league matches between the two clubs have seen Palace record 13 victories, to just four for Norwich, with six draws. As much as Palace might be the Canaries' 'bogey' side now, it has been a meeting of two halves, as the positions were reversed previously, putting Norwich on 14, Palace four with five draws. The clubs have now met competitively on 104 occasions; all but four have been on league business, the remaining four games all FA Cup ties; three of those (one went to a replay) being played before World War II. The two clubs met on the opening day of the Premiership season on August 14th 2004, playing out a 1-1 draw, with Darren Huckerby scoring for Norwich. It is a sobering thought that, if Norwich had not conceded Andrew Johnson's 73rd-minute equaliser on that day, and gone on to win 1-0, they would have avoided relegation that season by one point, sending West Bromwich Albion down instead. Johnson's strike (in hindsight!) turned out to be one of the most costly ever conceded by the club.

THE JOY OF SELHURST

JUST 8,369 fans turned out to see Norwich win 2-1 at Crystal Palace on February 25th 1986, as Norwich recorded their tenth consecutive league victory. The side on that day was Woods, Culverhouse, Deehan, Bruce, Phelan, Watson, Barham, Drinkell, Biggins, Mendham and Williams. Wayne Biggins and Peter Mendham scored for Norwich, the day ending with Norwich six points clear of Portsmouth at the top of the Division Two table.

CONTRASTS

ON January 5th 1980, Norwich, fifth in League Division One, and unbeaten at home, travelled to non-league Yeovil Town and their famous sloping pitch for an FA Cup third-round tie that had all the makings of a giant-killing, complete with BBC cameras, eagerly featuring the game for *Match Of The Day* that evening. Yeovil, then occupying tenth position in the English Conference, had lost their previous league fixture, at Weymouth, 3-0, their third defeat in a row, but confidence was high at The Huish, and bullish statements were issued from the Yeovil camp in the days leading up to the game, mostly of the 'they don't like it up 'em' variety. Norwich, however, won convincingly 3-0, the goals coming from Justin Fashanu, Graham Paddon and Keith Robson. Norwich went on to win their next league fixture, a home clash with Coventry City, by 1-0 (Robson's fourth goal in five starts), moving up to fourth in the First Division, whilst Yeovil played Gravesend & Northfleet a fortnight later, losing 2-0, and dropping to 12th in the Conference. It was, and remains, clear that there was a tremendous gulf between the two clubs at that time, but, such is the beauty of football that, a few weeks short of 30 years later, on December 12th 2009, the two teams met at Yeovil as footballing equals, in a Division One league match, with only nine league places (rather than 100) separating the two clubs at kick-off, a game that ended in a 3-3 draw, with both teams scoring their third goals in injury time, Gary Doherty's last gasp equaliser for Norwich coming in the 95th minute.

ADAMS AT THE MIKE

BBC radio Norfolk co-commentator Neil Adams is well placed to pass comment on Norwich games, having had a 16 year career in the game that included winning a league championship winners' medal with Everton in 1987. He joined Norwich from Everton for a fee of £250,000 in June 1994, swiftly establishing himself in the team as an attacking midfielder and wide player, as well as penalty taker par excellence. In total, he made 206 appearances for Norwich, scoring 30 goals. Adams combines his media duties with coaching the Norwich under-14 team and is a well respected coach, and holder of the Uefa 'A' licence, the second-highest coaching qualification in the modern game.

HOME AND AWAY

THE closest English league ground to Carrow Road is Portman Road, home of long-time East Anglian rivals Ipswich Town. Ipswich is 44 miles from Norwich. The longest away trip for club and fans is to Plymouth Argyle's Home Park ground, with Plymouth 360 miles from Norwich. Most City fans would regard Brunton Park, HQ of Carlisle United to be the most remote outpost for the Canaries to travel, however, the distance from Norwich to Carlisle is 'only' 282 miles, a short trip, compared to that long haul to Plymouth!

BOY DUBLIN GOOD

NORWICH released teenage centre-back Dion Dublin in 1988 before he had an opportunity to play in the first team. Dublin went on to sign for Cambridge United, and, in four years at the club, scored 52 goals in 156 league games. This attracted the attention of Manchester United, who signed him for £1 million in August 1992, supposedly as an alternative to Alan Shearer, who had snubbed United in favour of Blackburn Rovers. Sadly, Dublin broke his leg early in his Old Trafford career, and, by the time he had regained full fitness, had to contend with Eric Cantona for a first-team place. Dublin moved to Coventry City, and following later spells at Aston Villa, Leicester City and Celtic, signed for Norwich, at the age of 37, in September 2006, nearly two decades after the club had released him. Dublin's return to Norwich was a success all round as he scored 16 goals in 79 appearances helping the club avoid relegation from the Championship in the 2007/08 season, and, following his retirement (it had been hoped he would stay for one further season) that May, he was deservedly awarded the Barry Butler Memorial trophy for Player of the Year.

O'NEILL CAPPED

MARTIN O'Neill made 18 appearances for Northern Ireland during his two spells at the club between 1981 and 1983, including all five of their games at the 1982 World Cup finals in Spain – the most made by a Norwich player at that level. When he rejoined Norwich from Manchester City in February 1982, the entire £125,000 fee was deducted from the money City still owed Norwich for signing Kevin Reeves two years earlier!

YOU'VE BEEN ROBB'D

NORWICH paid Aberdeen £10,000 for the energetic forward Davie Robb in September 1978, no doubt hoping that he would form a formidable partnership with Kevin Reeves. Robb certainly looked the part on his debut, scoring and playing well in the Canaries' 3-0 home win over Derby County, a game that was one of the club's rare features on BBC TV's *Match of the Day*, garnishing John Bond's attack-minded team with a good reputation and eighth place in the Division One table. Robb, however, was substituted in each of his next two games, and didn't get picked again until the Carrow Road clash with Bolton on February 3rd 1978, coming on as substitute to replace Justin Fashanu. He then started the following week in the return match against Derby County at the Baseball Ground. There were no similar heroics from either Robb or the team, with the match ending 1-1. By now, Fashanu was beginning to settle into the team and was forming a striking partnership with Reeves so Robb was quickly and quietly shipped out, joining Philadelphia Fury in the USA. Robb therefore joined ex-England striker Martin Chivers as a player who had joined Norwich that season with much expected of him, and scoring on his debut, only to disappoint and leave the club before the following spring.

OLD FARM SUCCESS

A CLASH against fierce East Anglian rivals Ipswich Town would hardly be the most pressure-free environment for any player making his debut for Norwich, much less if it was to be played at Portman Road, with three points perhaps putting your new club at the top of the table. However, the task in hand was easy for striker Leon McKenzie. He scored both goals in Norwich's 2-0 win on December 21st 2003, with the victory taking them to the top of the Championship, a position they remained in for the rest of that season. McKenzie showed his forte for scoring in the big matches again the following season, when, in the Carrow Road clash against Manchester United, he scored the second, earning the ultimately doomed City a memorable 2-0 win. McKenzie was therefore expected to score the goals that would get Norwich back into the Premiership following relegation. His latter time at the club was troubled by injury, and he joined Coventry City in August 2006.

CAN'T WIN, WON'T WIN

NORWICH'S longest run of league games without a win came in the 1956/57 season, when the team went from September 22nd 1956 to February 23rd 1957, 25 league games in all, without a solitary league victory. The same period also represents the longest run the club has ever had in failing to keep a clean sheet. By any standards, the club's woes on the pitch during that time were spectacular. Out of a possible 50 league points up for grabs in that run of games, they only managed to get nine, and there were many heavy defeats, including 5-1 at Millwall, 6-3 at Walsall, 5-2 at home to Reading (this was a week after the slaughter at Walsall) and a 7-1 annihilation at Torquay United! Surprisingly, the goalkeeper for much of that run, including those heavy defeats, was Ken Nethercott, later to become an FA Cup hero for the club, but, at that time, the man who let in 41 goals in just 14 games. The defeat at Torquay United was Nethercott's last game that season for the club, and he didn't appear in a league game again until November in the following season. Ken Oxford had started the season as first choice goalkeeper and he retained his place after the Torquay match until the end of the season. The run was not just restricted to the league and any hopes that the club might have had of some distraction in the FA Cup were brought to an abrupt halt by non-league Bedford Town who came to Carrow Road as underdogs in the first-round tie on November 17th, only to secure a shock (well, maybe not much of a shock) 4-2 win. The rot finally came to an end on March 2nd 1957 with some revenge over Millwall, goals by Peter Gordon and Billy Coxon securing a 2-0 victory, with a 5-4 win at Shrewsbury Town following in the next match, future Wolves boss Sammy Chung scoring two of the goals. The season was best forgotten at its end and Norwich ended it bottom of the Division Three (South) table, the agony suitably honed by the fact that Ipswich Town ended up as champions! For two Norwich players the season had marked some moderate personal success; forwards Johnny Gavin and Ralph Hunt still managed to score 36 goals between them, the former being the only player that season to appear in all of the club's league games, as well as that FA Cup defeat.

WOODS OF ENGLAND

NORWICH found it difficult to replace legendary goalkeeper Kevin Keelan after he played his final game for the club in February 1980. Roger Hansbury and Clive Baker were immediate rivals for his place, Hansbury initially taking the number one shirt, playing in all of the Canaries' remaining matches of that season, a total of 16 league appearances, during which time he conceded 28 goals, including four in his first appearance, as City, fresh from a 5-3 home defeat to Liverpool (Keelan's final game) shipped in another four, this time in a 4-0 humbling at Wolves. John Bond had faith in Hansbury and he repaid it by keeping a clean sheet in his next two games; 0-0 draws against Middlesbrough and Manchester City. Hansbury duly kept the shirt for the start of the 1980/81 season, losing his place to Baker midway through the campaign, regaining the shirt, and then losing it again following the signing of ex-Forest keeper Chris Woods from QPR for £225,000 in March 1981. Woods made his debut in the 3-0 defeat at Wolves, and played for the rest of that season, conceding nine goals in as many games as the club were eventually relegated to Division Two. City went straight back up again the following campaign, and Woods was an ever-present, playing in all 48 league and cup games, as he did again in the following two seasons, making 170 consecutive appearances for the club in that time. He eventually missed out in the 3-1 defeat, ironically, against Nottingham Forest, on September 29th 1984 – Manchester City and ex-England keeper Joe Corrigan joined the club on loan to cover for Woods – and the following two games, but still played in 38 of Norwich's 42 league games that season. He also featured in all of their cup appearances, culminating in winning a second League Cup winners' medal, as City defeated Sunderland, 1-0, at Wembley. The season should have been a personal triumph for Woods as he went on to make his England debut that summer, but, despite his fine performances all season, Norwich were relegated. Woods was, once again, an ever-present in the Norwich side that won promotion back to Division One at the end of the 1985/86 season, conceding just 37 goals in 42 league matches – the joint lowest in Division Two that season. He was not, however, destined to play for Norwich at the highest level again and joined Rangers that summer for £600,000, his place in the hearts of Norwich fans ensured.

ROBSON SACKED!

SIR Bobby Robson's last home match as Newcastle United manager was the Premiership fixture against Norwich City on August 25th 2004. The Canaries came back from a 2-0 deficit to draw the game 2-2, with goals by David Bentley and Gary Doherty. Following defeat in their next game to Aston Villa, Robson was unceremoniously sacked by Newcastle United.

MILKY TEARS

NORWICH were the first team to win a game on Luton Town's infamous plastic pitch, the victory coming in a Milk Cup game in 1985 with goals from Peter Mendham and Steve Bruce securing a 2-0 win. Upon Norwich's return to the First Division the next season, both league games in that 1986/87 season finished as 0-0 draws, the game at Luton on October 11th earning City the point that took them to the top of the First Division table for the first and only time that season, Norwich eventually finishing fifth.

BUTTS' FIRST GOAL

CENTRAL defender Ian Butterworth joined Norwich from Nottingham Forest in 1986, scoring his first Norwich goal in January 1989 in a league game at Millwall. Nothing too unusual the casual fan might think about that, but it was quite a game, and quite an occasion as well, televised live by ITV. Before the game, Norwich were in second spot in the First Division, six points behind leaders Arsenal, and making an unlikely title challenge under Dave Stringer. All looked well for the Canaries as they raced into an early 2-0 lead, Mark Bowen scoring the second after just seven minutes to momentarily silence a typically noisy and passionate crowd at The Den. However, with Teddy Sheringham and Jimmy Carter starting to make an impact on the game, Millwall brought the score back to 2-2 and would have won, had it not been a series of heroic saves by Bryan Gunn. With Butterworth and his fellow defenders severely under the cosh, Norwich needed to ease the pressure in any way they could just to preserve the draw. However, they did so in style! A cross into the Millwall penalty area was partially cleared, the ball falling to Scottish international striker Robert Fleck whose exquisite volley won the game, consolidating City's second place and challenge to Arsenal.

THE 'BIG' FOUR?

THE 1986/87 season, Norwich's first back in the old First Division after promotion the previous campaign, saw them show no fear in their games against the clubs now known in English football as the 'Big Four'. In their eight league games against Arsenal, Chelsea, Liverpool, and Manchester United, Norwich drew four – home to Arsenal and Manchester United, home and away against Chelsea – and won three – home to Liverpool, and, impressively, away at Arsenal and Manchester United. The only defeat was a 6-2 thrashing at Liverpool. Other opponents for Norwich that season were clubs that have since descended all the way to non-league football; Luton Town, Wimbledon and Oxford United. Norwich lost at Wimbledon by 2-0 in October 1986, the week before that defeat at Liverpool, and one of only two occasions the club lost two consecutive league games that season. The eventual Football League champions that season were Everton, complete with ex-Canaries skipper Dave Watson in their ranks. Watson would have enjoyed the two games against his old club, helping to keep two clean sheets with Everton winning 4-0 at Goodison Park, and 1-0 at Carrow Road.

BIG JOHN

JOHN Fashanu, better known as a fearsome striker for Wimbledon, including making two unlikely appearances for England, and, perhaps even more famous for his stint on *I'm a Celebrity, Get Me Out Of Here* in 2003, as well as co-presenting ITV's *Gladiators* with Ulrika Jonsson, began his football career with Norwich. He appeared in just seven league games, scoring on his full home league debut, the 4-1 win over Derby County on November 21st 1981. Norwich won only two of their consequent ten league matches, and were as low as 13th in the table, following the 1 1 draw at Orient on March 16th 1982. A run of ten victories in their final 12 matches secured third place and promotion. Fashanu remained at the club for the following season back in the First Division, his first-ever top-flight appearance coming in the 1-1 draw at Everton on September 18th 1982. His final game was the following week against West Bromwich Albion at Carrow Road, starting, but later replaced by Phil Alexander (Alexander's only appearance for the club!), as Norwich lost 3-1. Fashanu joined Lincoln City a year later, scoring 11 goals in 36 league games for the Imps.

WORLD CUP FEVER

ENGLAND'S bid to host the 2018 World Cup was never likely to see a submission from Norwich to have Carrow Road as one of the tournament's host stadia. But, when England first hosted the tournament in 1966, there were hopes that the ground would have been one of those used. A sum of £33,000 was required to up the capacity of the existing stadium to 48,000, a figure that was eventually declared as unrealistic for practical and safety reasons. To date, Carrow Road has never staged a full international fixture, although, with ambitious plans to increase the capacity to 35,000-plus, there is no reason why the ground should not hold important matches in the future.

ENGLAND U-21'S

DESPITE Carrow Road never having held a full international match, the England under-21 team has played there on three occasions. The first was in 1983, when the team beat their Danish counterparts 4-1. Norwich had to wait 14 years for their next turn to host an under-21 match, beating Greece 4-2 in 1997, a match distinguished by the fact it was the first and only appearance made by Michael Owen for the under-21s. Finally, in 2007, England under-21s beat Slovakia under-21s 5-0 in a friendly, watched by an impressive Carrow Road crowd of just over 20,000; future Norwich loanees Leroy Lita and Ben Alnwick being part of the England squad on the night.

BERTHEL OF JUTLAND

NORWICH'S Belgian defender Jens Berthel Askou began his professional career at minor Danish club Holstebro BK, who are situated in West Jutland. Askou played for them in 2002/03 before joining Silkeborg IF in 2003, and helping them win promotion back to the Danish Superliga in his first season.

CURETON'S BOW

THIRTEEN years spanned striker Jamie Cureton's two debuts for Norwich. His first league appearance for the club was against Everton in November 1994, then, following a subsequent career at seven different clubs, he returned to Carrow Road, making his second 'debut' in a Carling Cup tie against Barnet in August 2007, scoring twice.

MANAGERIAL CHANGES

THE commencement of the 2009/10 season would have been only the fifth campaign that Jamie Cureton began at Carrow Road. Less than a month into that season, he was already playing for his ninth manager with the appointment of Paul Lambert. Prior to Lambert's arrival, he had played under John Deehan, Martin O'Neill, Gary Megson, Mike Walker (first spell) then Peter Grant, Jim Duffy (caretaker), Glenn Roeder and Bryan Gunn. Illustrating the relative stability at football clubs in 'times gone by', it is interesting to note above that, in his 17-year career at Norwich, goalkeeper Kevin Keelan played for just four; Ron Ashman, Lol Morgan, Ron Saunders and John Bond.

DEBUT HYSTERIA

DEBUTANT Simon Ratcliffe must have wondered what all the fuss was about when he made his Norwich City bow against Newcastle United on September 1st 1987; such was the media interest in the game. Neither the international or national TV and press crews attending Carrow Road were interested in Ratcliffe, a free signing from Manchester United. Their interest was in Brazilian international Mirandinha, making his Newcastle debut. Mirandinha had been touted as the first Brazilian to play in English football, disregarding the fact that Brazilian-born Edward Laxton had made his Norwich debut, against Plymouth Argyle, nearly 70 years earlier!

NORWICH'S CHARLTON

DEFENDER Simon Charlton was signed by Norwich prior to their Premiership return in 2004/05, flying out to join his new teammates in Malaysia following his £250,000 capture from Bolton Wanderers. He made 50 appearances for the club in two seasons, filling a number of different positions under Nigel Worthington, and finding it difficult to establish himself in his preferred position of left-back, such was the fine form of Adam Drury. He did appear in 24 of Norwich's games in that Premiership season, scoring in a 2-2 Carrow Road draw against Portsmouth on October 2nd, his first goal in nine years! His only other goal for the club came as a makeshift midfielder, in the club's 2-1 Carrow Road success over Burnley on December 28th 2005 in the Football League Championship.

PREMIERSHIP FAVOURITES?

AS thoughts started to turn to Christmas in early December 1992, Norwich led the Premiership table by an astonishing eight points after 18 games. The top of that table, after the games played on 5th December was as follows:

		P	W	D	L	GF	GA	PTS	GD
1.	Norwich City	18	12	3	3	34	31	39	+3
2.	Blackburn Rovers	18	8	7	3	28	15	31	+13
3.	Aston Villa	18	8	7	3	28	19	31	+9
4.	Chelsea	18	9	4	5	26	20	31	+6

DESPITE this huge lead, manager Mike Walker refused to get carried away, announcing that the club needed just a few more wins to be sure of avoiding relegation, perhaps suggesting that the club's success at that time had taken him by surprise even more than the rest of the football supporting country!

BIG DUNC

IN the 1970s, it seemed that every team had a 'hard man' defender whose role included roughing up opposing players, especially those that had the temerity to venture near his exclusive territory. Norwich were no exception, and, for the whole of that decade could rely upon Duncan Forbes to do just that. Born in Edinburgh in 1941, Forbes joined Norwich from Colchester United for just £10,000 in 1968, going on to make 357 appearances for the club. Whilst not exactly a physical giant, Forbes was a shade under six feet and weighed around 11 and a half stone in his playing days. Forbes' very presence pervaded Carrow Road, his distinctive and strong voice often heard on the pitch above the game. Forbes skippered the club to two promotions and two League Cup finals, making his debut in a 3-1 victory at Fulham on September 12th 1968, scoring his first goal (whilst wearing an unfamiliar number 11 shirt!) in another away success, 2-1 at Aston Villa, on December 21st. He replaced Ken Mallender as captain in the league game at Millwall the following season, City losing that game 1-0. His last game for Norwich was the 1-1 Carrow Road draw with Wolves on October 11th 1980.

THE MAJOR

MAJOR Frank Buckley spent a short time as Norwich manager from 1919/20, guiding the club to a notable, if not national, early cup success in the Norwich Hospital Cup via a 2-1 win over Birmingham. With a trophy secured, both Norwich and their new manager looked forward to the 1919/20 season with some optimism. Sometimes optimism is misguided. Buckley's fondness for wheeling and dealing saw Norwich use 40 different players that season, it wasn't only the dressing room that was crowded, for, at that time, Norwich had 12 board members, all it seems, at odds with one another. Many clashed over the financial affairs of the club, and after a succession of key players left, Buckley quit the club, eventually taking over at Blackpool, before taking over at Wolves in 1927. He went on to win the Second Division title with them in 1932, runners-up in the First Division in 1938, and again in 1939, when Wolves were also runners-up in the FA Cup. Later on in his managerial career, Buckley took over at Leeds United, being responsible for developing their youth talent, including the footballing genius that was John Charles. His legacy is perhaps the fact that many of the features he introduced to clubs during his time with them, regarded as innovatory at the time, are now considered the norm. These include special diets and training regimes for players, as well as the introduction and development of youth policies, something that might well have benefitted Norwich at the time, had the club's directors been better able to relate to his methods.

THE BEST

NORWICH'S first game after the departure of Ron Saunders was against Manchester United at Old Trafford on November 24th 1973. George Best featured in the United team on the day, but only showed flashes of his skill as the game ended 0-0, United ultimately joining Norwich in Division Two at the end of the season. Norwich interviewed Bournemouth boss John Bond for the vacant manager's job directly after the game; the Cherries having beaten Charlton Athletic 1-0 in the FA Cup first round on the same day.

A BADGE IS HATCHED!

THE first Norwich club badge to feature a Canary was introduced in 1922.

FERRARI FOR NORWICH!

NORWICH City have had their very own Ferrari, although it (or rather he) wasn't at the club for very long! Centre-back Fred Ferrari made four appearances for the club in their 1927/28 Division Three (South) season, having joined from Welsh side Flint for the princely sum of £150. The last of those games was less than a month later, a 2-2 draw at home to Exeter City. Ferrari went on to play for Barrow and Nelson. A more modern Ferrari currently residing at Carrow Road is Joe Ferrari, the club's head of media, a role and job description that would have been beyond the imagination of Fred Ferrari and the Norwich City team of the time!

YELLOW AND GREEN

NORWICH City do not just wear green as part of their kit, the club are also very aware of their responsibilities to the environment, the club programme being printed using paper from sustainable sources. The club have also introduced its own 'Yellow and Greener Day' in recent years, further highlighting the club's commitment to the environment, including reducing the amount of waste that used to be sent to landfill by installing recycling facilities around the ground, and at the Colney training complex.

DISTINGUISHED

JOHN Church played for Norwich from 1938 to 1950. His career at the club (114 appearances, 16 goals – including three goals in three minutes against Crystal Palace in a minor cup match), was interrupted by the outbreak of World War II. During the conflict, Church served as a different type of sharpshooter with the Royal Marine Commandos, being awarded the DSM during the conflict. He resumed his career with the club in the opening game of the 1946/47 season which saw Norwich beat Cardiff City 2-1.

IT'S ZAMORA

FULHAM'S Bobby Zamora, like Dion Dublin, is an example of a player proving Norwich City wrong after being released by the club. However, City were not the first club to let Zamora go cheaply when he left in 1996; he had previously been released by both West Ham United and Chelsea.

MR PRESIDENT

EVEN the self-proclaimed leaders of the free world have played for Norwich City. Well, their namesakes have! Charles Reagan, rather than US President Ronald, wore the Norwich shirt from 1954 to 1956, making 36 appearances for the club, scoring on his debut in the Canaries' 4-3 win over Aldershot on the opening day of the 1954/55 season. His acting abilities are unknown. Alfred Ford, namesake of Gerald the one-term wonder, was a one-game equivalent for Norwich in 1924 – a 2-2 home draw against Reading on the last day of the 1923/24 season. Like Gerald, he swiftly vanished into obscurity, ending up at Peterborough and Fletton United. President John F. Kennedy was famously assassinated in 1963, and, in Celtic loanee, John Kennedy, Norwich had their very own man of that name, one whose career was sadly interrupted and eventually ended by injury (if not so dramatically as his namesake's); Norwich's very own JK made 16 appearances for the club before his recurring knee injury ended his career in 2009. Woodrow Wilson led America through World War I, ending his presidency in 1921, three years before Joseph Wilson, a footballing, rather than political left-winger, made his debut for Norwich. Wilson (P.) went on to make a further 40 appearances for the Canaries. Delving further back into history, Ulysses S. Grant led the United States for eight years from 1869 to 77, having a rather more successful period at the helm than Norwich manager Peter Grant, whose own period in charge at the club was for just under a year, from 2006 to 2007. Sadly, the Canaries have yet to field an Obama, or, perhaps more fortunately, a Bush. However, the latter's predecessor Bill Clinton came dangerously close to having a Canaries equivalent, forward Paul Clayton being the nearly man here, in a similar fashion to his Norwich career, making just 15 appearances between 1983 and 1988.

MILBURN BROTHERS

OF the four famous footballing Milburn brothers, it is Jackie, of Newcastle United and England, who is the most well known. His older brother John, who also had a good career, primarily with Leeds United, played for Norwich at the end of the 1938/39 season, making 15 league appearances including one against 'Wor' Jackie's future team, the fixture against Newcastle United on March 16th ending in a 1-1 draw. Fellow Geordie Billy Furness scored the Norwich goal.

EXPENSIVE LIGHTING!

ONE of the highlights of the largely unforgettable 1956/57 season was the arrival of the club's floodlights, the installation of which was celebrated with a friendly game against Division One giants Sunderland, Norwich gallantly, but ultimately, losing 3-0. Significantly more worrying than that first floodlit performance, was the fact that purchase and installation of those floodlights turned out to be an investment that the club could not afford. The total cost exceeded £9,000, and, following an FA Cup humiliation against non-league Bedford in November 1956, it was announced that the club were not able to find enough cash to pay the players' and club staff's wages, and was on the very brink of extinction. It was only an act of some considerable generosity that the club survived, with the forerunner of current Norwich-based publishing company Archant. The Norwich News Company lent the club enough money to ensure its immediate future. It was obvious; a new approach was needed to ensure the club's long-term survival. A meeting was held on Monday 7th January 1957 (two days earlier City had drawn 2-2 against Walsall, a game that saw Terry Bly score his first Carrow Road goal) which ultimately led to the appointment of Mr Geoffrey Watling as chairman, the new board's intention under his leadership being to raise the not inconsiderable sum of £25,000 as well as swiftly putting matters right on the pitch. Under Watling's guidance, the amount was raised before the end of the season, and the club was saved.

SIR GEOFFREY WATLING

WATLING remained as chairman of Norwich until 1973, when he stood down for health reasons. Under his stewardship, the club had survived periods of tremendous financial instability, and, ultimately, with Ron Saunders, a Watling appointment, as manager, reached the First Division for the first time in their history. He came to the club's aid again in 1996, purchasing the shares held by then City chairman Robert Chase upon his departure from the club, selling them on to Delia Smith and Michael Wynn-Jones, and, in doing so, securing the future of the club he loved for a second time. Should Norwich ever follow the tradition of erecting a statue outside the ground of one of the club 'greats', there are many who would see Watling as an outstanding candidate for that honour.

GOING FOR BROOKE

WHEN Norwich signed Tottenham midfielder Garry Brooke in May 1985, they had a player who had won FA Cup and Uefa Cup winners' medals, with Spurs, and, at just 24, was tipped for a bright future in the game. The signing of Brooke was testimony to Ken Brown's powers of persuasion. City had just dropped down into the Second Division and following the Heysel tragedy, there would be no European campaign for Brooke to look forward to. He joined fellow new signing and midfielder David Williams, who, at 30, and having spent the previous ten years of his career at Bristol Rovers, was expected to settle for a place as a squad member. Brooke was anticipated as an established first-team member and a potential star in the making. However, this proved to be far from being the case. In 1985/86, the Canaries' returned to the First Division as Williams appeared in 39 of the team's 42 league games, scoring 8 goals, including one in a crucial 2-0 win at Sunderland. In all, Williams appeared in all but six of the Canaries 53 games that season, including being an ever-present during their run in the Screen Sport Super Cup – he scored in this competition too, against Manchester United. Brooke, in contrast, had a disappointing season. He appeared in the opening game of the campaign, a turgid 1-0 Carrow Road victory over Oldham Athletic, and scored in his third appearance, a 4-2 defeat at Millwall. After playing in the following match, a 1-1 home draw with Barnsley, he didn't appear again until the Canaries' 11th game of the season, replacing Tony Spearing as Norwich lost 2-1 to Wimbledon. Brooke played, and scored, in the next game, an impressive 4-0 win at Carlisle United, but, out of the remaining 30 league games, Brooke only started three, coming on as a substitute in a further four, and being selected as a non-playing substitute in another ten. He had been unable to oust Williams from the side, but, perhaps that was not too surprising, as Williams provided stealth and guile in the Canaries midfield, whilst Brooke was all about energy and commitment. Even in this role, Brooke could not displace Peter Mendham, whose 35 league appearances and eight goals spoke volumes for his ability. Brooke left Norwich during the following season, whilst Williams went on to play for the Canaries in Division One, for Wales, and eventually in a senior coaching capacity with the club.

HENRI LOSS

NORWICH'S 2010/11 loan signing Henri Lansbury is seen as one of the better prospects in Arsene Wenger's young squad, backed up by his signing a long term contract with the club towards the end of 2009. Lansbury, a midfielder, spent much of the 2009/10 season on loan under former Norwich stalwart Malkay Mackay at Watford. He made his Arsenal debut at the age of 17, however, Lansbury started at Norwich as a schoolboy, leaving the club for Arsenal when he was only nine years old. Another Norwich youngster who left for the bright lights of London at that very early age was Lansbury's future Arsenal teammate, Jay Simpson, who is spending the 2009/10 season on loan at QPR before joining Hull City.

LOAN STAR RYAN

OF all Norwich's numerous loan signings in the period from 2007-09, one of the most impressive and consistent was Chelsea left-back Ryan Bertrand. Bertrand, who has represented England at U-17, 19, 20 and 21 level had been on loan at Oldham Athletic before Norwich manager Glenn Roeder signed him in January 2008. He made 18 league appearances up until the end of that season, and, following his re-joining Norwich for the 2008/09 season, made 38 league appearances as the Canaries unsuccessfully battled relegation from the Championship. Up until the end of 2009, Bertrand had not made a single league appearance for Chelsea, but, in the space of just over three years, had made over 100 league appearances for five different league clubs, Bournemouth, Oldham Athletic, Reading and Nottingham Forest being the other clubs he has represented.

TEN FOR CITY

NORWICH'S record league win, a 10-2 home romp against Coventry City on March 15th 1930, hardly came on the back of a good run of form. The Canaries had only won one of their previous five league games, and their first league encounter at Coventry that season, the previous November, had seen them slump to a 3-1 defeat. Thomas Hunt led the way during that remarkable return fixture win, scoring five of Norwich's goals. Any thoughts of a late push for promotion that season came to a swift end the following Saturday, when, leading 1-0 at Watford at half-time, albeit via an own goal, Norwich eventually lost 2-1.

BUCKING THE TREND

WHEN Norwich played Chelsea at Carrow Road in a Premiership fixture on March 5th 2005, the side that took on Jose Mourinho's league of nations line up (featuring players from Portugal, the Czech Republic, the Ivory Coast and France) was solely British. Of the starting line up, ten of the Canaries players that day were English, Scottish international Gary Holt being the sole exception. The Norwich side was as follows; Green, Edworthy, Drury, Fleming, Shackell, Holt, Huckerby, McKenzie, Ashton, Francis, and Stuart. Sadly, Nigel Worthington's penchant for home-grown players for that game did not mean a great patriotic victory for his team, and Norwich lost 3-1. One player did make his mark on that day; Leon McKenzie's goal being the first conceded in the Premiership by Chelsea keeper Petr Cech in 1,025 minutes – a new record.

LEAGUE CUP WINNERS

THE League Cup wasn't taken quite as seriously in its early days as it is now. Despite that, Norwich refused to let that fact get in the way of the club's celebrations in winning the competition in only its second season, 1961/62. The club's first campaign in that trophy, the previous season, had seen them have convincing second- and third-round victories over Oldham Athletic (6-2, Bunny Larkin and Brian Whitehouse scoring a brace each) and 4-1 over fellow Second Division side Derby County, before surprisingly going out, 1-0 at Shrewsbury Town in the fourth round. In that ultimately victorious season, City got through the first four rounds at the first attempt, with wins over Chesterfield (3-2), Lincoln City (3-2), Middlesbrough (3-2) and future final opponents, Sunderland (4-1). The first leg of the semi-final against Blackpool resulted in a convincing 4-1 win in front of nearly 20,000 success-starved fans, and, although Norwich lost the second leg, 2-0, they advanced into the final 4-3 on aggregate. The Canaries' opponents were to be Rochdale, who, at the time of the first leg at Spotland, were 14th in Division Four having lost three of their last four league games. Norwich duly triumphed 3-0, Derrick Lythgoe scoring twice with Bill Punton scoring the other. A gate of 19,800 attended the second leg at Carrow Road a week later, with Norwich winning 1-0, a second-half goal by Jimmy Hill ensuring that first major cup success.

TERRY BLY – CENTRE FORWARD

IN 1959, one of the most famous Norwich City teams in its history reached the semi-finals of the FA Cup – the first to do so as a Third Division side. The Canaries number nine during that cup run was Terry Bly. Wearing a number nine shirt at that time meant something to any footballer. It was not, as is now, just a squad number; it meant that you were the centre forward, the man who led the line and scored the goals. And scoring goals is what Terry Bly did, throughout a three-and-a-half year stay at Norwich that began when he signed from Bury Town in August 1956. It is difficult now to emphasise just how impressive that FA Cup run was. Football at that time saw no Champions League, no focus on who would finish in the top four, indeed, no-one spoke of a 'big four' when most of the teams in the top division were capable of winning it. In the 13 years between the resumption of competitive football in England (following World War II) and the 1958/59 season, seven different teams were crowned as First Division champions. In the FA Cup, over the same period, <u>eleven</u> different teams won the trophy. Competition, therefore, was fierce. There were many great teams and great players. The FA Cup meant as much to any footballer, club, manager or supporter, as the Champions League does now – probably more. Winning the league title, yes, that was an achievement. But to win the FA Cup? That was the pinnacle. So for Norwich City, who had finished the previous league season a distant eighth in the old Division Three (South), to come close to making the final of this competition was little less than a footballing miracle. To reach that FA Cup semi-final in 1959, Norwich played 11 games (a team can win it in six now!). Bly played in nine of them, scoring seven goals. In that same season, he scored 22 goals for Norwich – after making his first league appearance of that season on November 2nd 1958, against Notts County, a 3-3 draw. He missed the next three games before being recalled to the starting line-up in the home match against Southend United. Clearly keen to make a point, he scored. A hat-trick followed in the next league game as the Canaries thrashed QPR 5-1 at Carrow Road. A further nine goals followed in his next ten league games. Bly was swiftly becoming a local sensation.

IN the rather austere 1950s, a word such as 'sensation' was rarely used in sporting circles. Bly himself would never have acknowledged that fact. Modest, level-headed and a popular member of the squad, he saw scoring goals as his job, certainly not something that made him any more important than other members of the team. His stock was rising. In January 1959, Norwich faced Manchester United, the world famous 'Busby Babes' in the third round at Carrow Road. Many things have changed in football in these 50 years, but one thing was as constant as would be now – the expectation that the star-studded United side would have an easy victory over 'little old Norwich'. Norwich, under manager Archie Macaulay, had other thoughts and went into the game thinking they could win. If, therefore, they were not too surprised that they did win, then, surely the ease of their convincing 3-0 victory was rather more unexpected? Bly scored two of the goals, the second had Manchester United and Northern Ireland international goalkeeper Harry Gregg applauding him as the ball crashed into the back of his net to seal victory. What wouldn't Norwich give for a player of Bly's undoubted goalscoring ability now? And how much would he be worth, indeed, for how long would Norwich be able to hold onto him? Following that season – which saw Bly and the Norwich team finish fourth in the Division Three (South) – Bly scored another seven goals in 25 appearances as Norwich finished runners-up to Southampton, earning promotion to Division Two in the process for the first time in the club's history. Bly was not at the club in that initial Second Division season. In June 1960, newly elected to the Fourth Division, ambitious Peterborough United offered Norwich just £5,000 for him. The club accepted and Bly, still only 25 and yet to reach his peak, had gone. Why the club allowed him to leave could be seen as a lack of judgment, or, less politely, professionally irresponsible! Maybe some thought that his goalscoring prowess would not be repeated at a higher level, maybe others thought that he had peaked; seven goals in 25 games that year, and with some injury niggles, as opposed to his 22 goals in 23 league games the previous season. No doubt Bly took it all on the chin, said his goodbyes, politely accepted everyone's best wishes and just carried on doing what he did best: scoring goals.

IN his first season at Peterborough, he scored 52 goals and they were promoted. In that entire 42-game season back in 1960/61 the whole Norwich team only managed a further 18 goals than that. If anything, Bly exceeded his goalscoring exploits at Norwich during his time at Peterborough, scoring 81 goals in 88 appearances, before plundering a further 25 in 32 over just one season at Coventry City, before, in another puzzling move, Coventry manager Jimmy Hill sold him to Notts County where he saw out his football league career before eventually joining non-league Grantham. As ever, Bly was consistent, scoring on his debut and ending his first season with Grantham with four hat-tricks to his name. He will, however, always be primarily remembered, career-wise, for his contribution to that magnificent Canaries FA Cup run. Seven goals in nine games, the two against Manchester United, as well as a further brace against Sheffield United in the quarter-final replay win on March 4th. Just three days later, he scored another as Norwich beat Southampton in the league. Thus was the pattern of his football career; he played, he scored goals, and he did it with spectacular regularity, rightfully earning himself a place in the inaugural Canaries Hall of Fame. He passed away on September 4th 2009, aged 73, leaving behind precious memories of a Norfolk man and Norwich City player, whose football ability and modest, unassuming and likeable manner will never be forgotten by the club or its supporters.

BLY'S PARTNERS

DURING that FA Cup semi-final season, Bly's striking partners included Errol Crossan and Bobby Brennan. Brennan scored in Bly's debut game, the 3-3 draw against Notts County, with Crossan scoring the other two. Crossan scored 12 league goals in that season – as well as four in that FA Cup run – the same as Brennan. It is Brennan who remains the only Norwich City player to score for the club in an FA Cup semi-final, his equaliser against Luton Town earning the club a replay. Crossan scored an equally vital equaliser himself, against Sheffield United in the quarter-final. Bly and Brennan goals secured the 2-1 victory in that replay, thus setting up the semi-final at White Hart Lane against Luton Town where Brennan went on to make his little piece of Norwich City history.

THE 'Z' FACTOR

WHEN Houston-born centre-back Zak Whitbread joined Norwich from Millwall in January 2010, he became only the third Norwich City player to represent the club whose name began with a Z! Zema Abbey was the first, joining from Cambridge United in 2000, and spending an injury-hit four years with the Canaries, making 63 appearances, and scoring 8 goals. One of the more crucial strikes was a last-minute winner against then non-league Dagenham & Redbridge in an FA Cup fourth-round tie in 2003. Zesh Rehman, like Whitbread, a central defender, joined on loan from Fulham in 2006, making his debut against Ipswich on February 5th, Norwich losing 2-1. Another loanee, Charlton 'asset' Jonatan Johansson scored the Norwich goal. While at Fulham, Rehman became the first British Asian to start a Premiership match.

A GOOD CROWD!

IN the early years of Norwich City's existence, as the club plied its trade in the Norfolk & Suffolk, United, and Southern Leagues, attendances at their matches rarely – home or away – topped the 10,000 mark. The first example of a home match reaching that mark came on Christmas Day 1905 when 10,245 packed into Newmarket Road to witness the 1-0 festive success against Swindon Town in the club's first Southern League season, David Ross scoring the goal. In previous seasons, match attendances were not always recorded accurately. The gate figure for the return game at Swindon is not known (not that it matters, City won 3-1, David Ross again scoring) and, for their United League clash at home to Leyton on April 15th 1907, the attendance is recorded as 'few'. No-one missed very much, as the game was a 0-0 draw. In contrast to this, Norwich would certainly have been aware of the spectators in their FA Cup second-round match that same season, as 25,400 saw them narrowly lose 1-0 at West Bromwich Albion, the biggest crowd that the club had – at that point – played in front of, and one which they would not come anywhere near to matching at a home game until 1929. Just over 20,000 packed The Nest for another FA Cup tie, a third-round clash against Corinthians (the only time Norwich played against the famously maverick club) only to witness a 5-0 defeat as the sporting Corinthians defied tradition, and ran riot.

100 UP – 500 UP

NORWICH'S 100th game in top-flight English football was the 1-0 Carrow Road defeat against Middlesbrough on November 8th 1975, a young midfielder by the name of Graeme Souness scoring the Middlesbrough goal. The Canaries' 100th goal at this level came on 29th November 1975, Ted MacDougall's 89th-minute third in the 3-1 home win against Liverpool sealing that accolade. The club's 500th game in the top division came on April 20th 1987: a 1-1 draw at Nottingham Forest. Robert Rosario opened the scoring for the Canaries after 62 minutes, only for Nigel Clough to equalise. Mike Channon scored the 500th top-flight goal for Norwich, his 82nd-minute equaliser coming in the 2-1 defeat at Sunderland on 13th October 1984.

NOT QUITE 1,000 GAMES...

NORWICH have yet to play 1,000 games at the pinnacle of English league football. The Canaries' 864th, and, at present, final game in the top division was on 15th May 2005, a 6-0 capitulation at Fulham meaning that the team dropped back into the Championship after just one season.

BUT 1,000 GOALS? NO PROBLEM SIR

ONE bright spot of that disappointingly short return to the Premiership during the 2004/05 season, was the fact that club did manage to score its 1,000th goal at the highest level. The scorer was Darren Huckerby, a typically flamboyant effort earning the Canaries their consolation goal in the 4-1 defeat at Arsenal on April 2nd 2005.

THE 5,000TH!

MUCH of the Canaries' history has, of course, been spent outside of the elite in English football. Accordingly, the honour of the 5,000th league goal in all divisions for Norwich City falls to Welsh international Craig Bellamy, his sixth-minute penalty in the 4-2 win over QPR on August 2nd 1998 sealing his place in the Canaries' record book. The 5,001st came along just two minutes later. The scorer, against one of his former clubs, was defender Matt Jackson.

GOSS SCORES!

WELSH international midfielder Jeremy Goss shot to national fame during the 1993/94 Premiership season, mainly for his crucial (and spectacular) goals against Vitesse Arnhem and Bayern Munich in the club's famous Uefa Cup campaign under Mike Walker. Goss scored many notable goals in that season other than those that helped knock the Germans out of the competition. His first European goal was the second in the Canaries' 3-0 win over Vitesse Arnhem in the first round of the competition on September 15th. He also scored in the consecutive Premiership victories over Leeds United (4-0) and Ipswich (1-0) on August 21st and 25th. The goal at Elland Road, a stunning volley from a Ruel Fox cross, had the entire ground, Leeds fans included, on their feet and applauding. Three days after his half volley in front of the Barclay stand had drawn the Canaries level at 1-1 in that European tie, Norwich travelled north to Bramall Lane for a tough Premiership game against Sheffield United – a wake-up call after the glorious European triumph at Carrow Road. Many thought that this might be a game too far for the Canaries. Goss scored again in the 2-1 victory, securing the opener after less than half an hour, the understanding with Fox coming to the fore again as he headed home the winger's pinpoint cross. The victory maintained Norwich's second place in the Premiership table, and, once again, the team were being talked about as possible title winners. However, by the time Goss scored his next goal in that Premiership season – Norwich's third in an entertaining 3-3 draw at Swindon – Mike Walker had left the club and the Canaries had slipped to ninth in the league. His next goalscoring contribution was in another high-scoring game on April 9th, as Norwich lost 5-4 at Southampton, Goss's 48th-minute header temporarily putting the Canaries 2-1 up. He saved his last, and ninth goal of that eventful season, for Norwich's penultimate Premiership game, the trip to Liverpool on April 30th. What with this match being the last to be held in front of Liverpool's old Spion Kop, the setting for another of the Reds' traditional maulings of the men from Norfolk was truly set. In perhaps their best performance under the management of John Deehan, Norwich won 1-0 (and should have had more); Goss's exquisite 20-yard first-half volley is now in all the record books as the last-ever goal to be scored in front of that famous stand.

POOLS FAVOURITE

THE 1978/79 season saw Norwich a favourite pick for all football coupon fans. The reason for this was that out of their 42 league games, Norwich drew 23 of them, 13 of those being away fixtures. This meant that the club's away record for the season was quite decent – they lost only eight games – which was less than Arsenal, and only one more than rivals Ipswich, who finished sixth! They were also the only club not to win an away league match all season, and not only in the First Division, but in all four of the English leagues! They'd certainly had the chance to win an away game, or two. At Everton on March 30th two Kevin Reeves goals put the Canaries 2-0 up, which remained the score with less than half an hour to go. Mick Lyons equalised on 64 minutes, then, with only 4 minutes to go, hit the equaliser. Four weeks earlier Justin Fashanu put Norwich into a 2-1 lead at Leeds on the hour mark, only for John Hawley to immediately hit back for 2-2, which is how it remained. Perhaps the best chance of winning that elusive away game came at West Bromwich Albion back in September. City led 2-1 after going behind to a Laurie Cunningham goal, Martin Chivers and John Ryan scoring for Norwich. Yet, agonisingly, Bryan Robson demonstrated the tenacity that typified his career by scoring for the Baggies in injury time – 2-2 again. How different the season might have been for the Canaries had they held on in that match? At one point John Bond's men drew seven consecutive league fixtures, starting with a 0-0 at home to Arsenal on December 9th and lasting right the way through to the second week of February, and a 1-1 draw at Derby County, Martin Peters rescuing the now all-too-familiar point in the 85th minute. Clearly, something had to give, and it did the following week; the draw specialists travelled to Anfield where the nation's pools coupons were ruined as Norwich lost 6-0! That particular game was the last that Kevin Keelan played for a while, a broken thumb keeping him out for the rest of the season. Roger Hansbury stepped up and kept a clean sheet in his first game, a 1-0 Carrow Road victory over Middlesbrough, Martin Peters heading the winner. City duly saw out the season, safe enough from any relegation worries, and had at least won the devoted support of those for whom Norwich's one point meant they got three!

THREE AWAY POINTS AT LAST

NORWICH City commenced the 1979/80 campaign with a monkey on their backs. The previous three seasons had seen the team notch up exactly the same number of away victories – just three wins from 63 games. The Canaries' first league fixture of the new season was at Goodison Park where last time around Everton had equalised in the last five minutes to deny John Bond's team a long-awaited victory. The previous season had seen Norwich sent home on the back of a 3-0 defeat; future Norwich boss Bruce Rioch one of the Everton scorers. The one before that had seen Norwich lose 3-1, despite being ahead at half time. It was easy to understand therefore why the Norwich supporters heading to Merseyside were not expecting much, and the best result, yet another draw, was what most hoped for. However, in unexpected and 'typical Norwich' style, City rattled in four goals. Mick McGuire commenced the rout on ten minutes, Justin Fashanu added to his burgeoning reputation with a brace, with Martin Peters the other scorer. It was the club's first away success since the opening game two years previously, when West Ham United were beaten 3-1.

SUTTON'S QUARTER CENTURY

CHRIS Sutton scored 25 goals in 41 league appearances in the 1993/94 season, including a run of seven in eight games. Two of them came in an impressive 3-1 win at Tottenham Hotspur, a game which perfectly illustrated Mike Walker's attacking philosophy: Norwich had 15 shots on target!

PRIDE OF ANGLIA

NORWICH'S 13th-place finish in Division One in the 1977/78 season saw them end the season five places, and points, above near rivals Ipswich Town, the first time the Canaries had finished above them since 1966.

BLAIR'S BIG GAMES

SIGNED from St. Mirren, 1972, midfielder Jim Blair only made four starts for City in the 1972/73 season. Two of those matches were cup finals! The League Cup loss against Tottenham on March 3rd 1973, was followed by the second-leg defeat of the Texaco Cup Final against Ipswich on May 7th.

THE JONES BOYS

SIX players with the surname of Jones have represented Norwich over the years. The most well known is perhaps the last one to do so, Welsh international David Jones. He signed for Norwich from Nottingham Forest for £50,000 in September 1975, making his debut in the Canaries' 5-2 defeat at Newcastle United on October 18th, scoring Newcastle's fifth with an own goal. He missed the next three games, but, following his recall for the game against Coventry City on November 15th, missed only four more games that season. He commenced the following season partnering Duncan Forbes, starting in 35 of Norwich's 42 league games, scoring two goals, his first for the club in the opening game of the 1977/78 season, as Norwich beat West Ham United 3-1 – one of them a stunning 30-yard shot. He started a total of 128 league games for Norwich before injury ended his career in 1980. Jones is well known for being the innocent party in the infamous penalty incident that saw Wales lose out on a place in the 1978 World Cup finals, adjudged to have handballed when the real culprit was Scotland's Joe Jordan. The resultant penalty sealed Scotland's win and their place in Argentina.

CLOUGH SILENCED

NOTTINGHAM Forest won the league championship in 1978, following that up with two consecutive European Cup triumphs in 1979 and 1980 to, rightly, become one of the most feared and successful sides in Europe at that time, having also won the League Cup in 1978 and 1979. It is, therefore, a formidable side in the making, top of the table and on a 12-game unbeaten run that arrives at Norwich on September 15th 1979. Despite all that – and the fact that Peter Shilton had only conceded three goals in the preceding five league matches, and Forest had the likes of England international Tony Woodcock in attack, future Canary Martin O'Neill in midfield and Footballer of the Year Kenny Burns – and despite Brian Clough, Norwich won 3-1, knocking Forest off the top of the table in the process, whilst moving up to third place themselves. Norwich's three goals are scored in a magical spell of just under 20 minutes, with Kevin Reeves and Justin Fashanu (who would join Forest just under two years later) scoring towards the end of the first half, Keith Robson scoring the third on the hour mark.

SEMI-FINAL WOES

NORWICH'S best seasons in the FA Cup have seen them reach the semi-finals of the competition on three occasions. The first, and most famous, was the conclusion of their famous run in the trophy in 1959 when, after some stirring victories over the likes of Manchester United, Tottenham Hotspur and Sheffield United, they lost 1-0 in a semi-final replay to Luton Town. It took 30 years for the club to reach that stage for the second time – Sheffield United again one of the victims enroute – as an exciting fifth round tie at Carrow Road saw Norwich win 3-2, Dale Gordon scoring the winner. The semi-final, played at Villa Park against Everton resulted in a 1-0 defeat, a weakened Norwich side missing the influence of Phelan and the goal threat of Fleck; the day itself ultimately overshadowed by the tragic events in the other semi-final at Hillsborough. Three years later, Norwich were at Hillsborough themselves for their last, at present, appearance at the semi-final stage. This time their opponents, Sunderland, were from a lower division and Norwich were firm favourites. Fleck plays, but is clearly unfit, whilst Mark Walton replaced the injured Gunn in goal. John Byrne's 33rd-minute strike seals Sunderland's 1-0 victory as Norwich fail to impress, indeed, the defeat is a turning point in the Canaries' season as they go on to lose five of their last six matches, a dreary 1-1 home draw against Wimbledon the lone point during that run. League Cup semi-finals have been a somewhat luckier occasion, Norwich have played at that stage on five different occasions, winning through to the final in 1962, 1973, 1975, and 1985. However, their chances of reaching Wembley in the 1974 League Cup Final were thwarted by Wolves at the semi-final stage. Norwich had got that far by beating Wrexham, Everton (an impressive 1-0 win at Goodison Park on October 30th 1973, David Cross scoring), Southampton and Millwall, the 2-1 replay victory over the Lions drawing a lowly gate of just over 7,000 to Carrow Road. Cup fever was reignited for the first leg of that semi-final against Wolves with over 20,000 witnessing a 1-1 draw, Ian Mellor scoring his ninth and final goal for Norwich. Wolves shaded the second leg at Molineux, winning 2-1 on aggregate, and Norwich were denied a second consecutive trip to Wembley, although they made the final again the following season, defeating Manchester United 3-2 on aggregate at the semi-final stage.

CITIZEN MELLOR

LEFT-winger Ian Mellor joined Norwich from Manchester City in March 1973 for £65,000, scoring in only his third league game, a 3-1 defeat at Liverpool. He was a prolific goalscorer in cup games for Norwich, scoring three in the team's Texaco Cup run that same season, plus another four in five starts as the Canaries got to the League Cup semi-final the following year. He joined Brighton & Hove Albion in 1974 and is now a senior executive at the PFA.

KELLOCK'S EYE

FORWARD Billy Kellock scored in his first full appearance for Norwich, a 6-2 trouncing of Wrexham in a second-round League Cup tie in October 1973. That was pretty much it as far as his career in yellow and green was concerned; he made just two substitute appearances that season, his only start coming on April 13th 1974, the Canaries having one of their traditional thrashings in Merseyside on that day, 4-1 at Everton.

A BAD START

NORWICH had a terrible start to their 2000/01 Division One campaign, losing three of their first five games and scoring only two goals. The 0-0 draw at Crewe Alexandra on September 9th saw them slip to the bottom of the table as pressure mounted on manager Bryan Hamilton. He attempted to bring some experience and goalscoring expertise by signing ex-Leicester City, West Ham United, and Everton striker Tony Cottee and it seemed to pay off as he inspired Norwich to a 3-1 win at Stockport County in their next game, playing well alongside Iwan Roberts. Cottee seems to have the manager's ear, as, two games later, Steve Walsh also arrives from Leicester to take his place in the Canaries rearguard, having an immediate impact as Norwich lose 4-0 at Wolves. Neither Cottee nor Walsh hang around for long. Cottee cites the travelling from his London home as a reason for his departure after seven games to become manager of Barnet whilst Walsh, a tremendous player and leader whilst at his peak, had injury worries and was released at the beginning of 2001 after just five appearances. By now Hamilton has already gone, leaving after another defeat, 2-0 at Portsmouth on December 2nd, Norwich's tenth loss in just 20 games.

THE TALL GUY

AT 6ft 7ins. (2.0m), Peter Crouch is almost certainly the tallest player to have played for Norwich. He joined on loan from Aston Villa in September 2003, scoring on his debut, a 2-0 win over Burnley. As Crouch did a dance of delight with the River End, the much more diminutive Kevin Harper, himself a loan signing from Portsmouth, jumped on Crouch's back in celebration, hauling himself upwards as he did so – the resulting image being famously likened to 'a cat scaling a wardrobe'. Crouch made 15 appearances for Norwich in 2003, including getting a red card at Walsall, scoring four goals.

AND THE SHORT ONE

AMONG the more vertically modest players to have worn a small-sized shirt for Norwich City is Paul McVeigh, who tops out at 5ft 6ins. (1.67m). McVeigh originally played for Norwich from 2000 to 2007, appearing in 215 league games for the Canaries. He made his debut in a Division One game at Bolton on May 7th, coming on as a replacement for Cedric Anselin. Following a spell at Luton Town, McVeigh joined Norwich for a second time in the summer of 2009. He has made 20 appearances for Northern Ireland, 14 of those as a substitute.

BUSTER BROWN

A RELATIVELY short spell spent at Norwich for centre forward Oliver 'Buster' Brown from 1931 to 1933 saw him make just 51 league appearances. In that time, the ex-Nottingham Forest man scored 33 goals, including a hat-trick in just his third game as Norwich beat Watford 4-1. Consecutive braces against Bristol Rovers and Torquay United soon followed, Brown ending the season as second-highest Norwich goalscorer with 14 goals, despite having only played in 21 league games. During the following season, Brown scored seven goals in three league games, including four against Bournemouth as Norwich won 6-0; the team ultimately finishing third in the Division Three (South) and possibly missing out on a promotion spot due to Brown having missed 12 league games early in the season. He left the club to join West Ham United in the summer of 1933, and in 1934 when he was at Brighton & Hove Albion, topped their goalscoring list for 1933/34, despite only making a total of eight appearances!

CEDRIC ANSELIN

CEDRIC Anselin was the first of a clutch of French players who have ended up at Carrow Road in recent seasons. Big things were expected of the under-21 midfielder when he joined the club in 1999. Norwich had beaten off competition from Leeds United, Southampton and Middlesbrough to sign him, and the early signs were positive. Anselin made his debut and featured prominently in the 1-0 win at Grimsby on April 5th, a delicious Phil Mulryne free kick securing Norwich's first victory in nine games. His first goal followed in a 4-2 win at Oxford United, lobbing the U's keeper from 30 yards. It did all look very good for both Anselin and Norwich as Bruce Rioch's rebuilt team finished the season in a respectable ninth place in Division One. Following Rioch's departure in March of the following season, Anselin failed to convince his successor, Bryan Hamilton, and only started two more games, being substituted in both, the latter being his final game for the club as Norwich lost 1-0 at Bolton Wanderers.

JEAN-YVES DE BLASSIS

DE BLASSIS, another midfielder, had signed from Red Star Paris in the summer of 1999, making his debut in the opening-day 1-1 draw at West Bromwich Albion, a game Anselin also appeared in, going on to make 26 league starts that season. Injury restricted his playing time in 2000/01 and he made just two league starts, eventually being released at the end of the season.

MARC LIBBRA

THE club maintained its French links at the beginning of the 2001/02 season, Nigel Worthington signing charismatic striker Libbra after a protracted chase that summer. Libbra had spent a short time at Hibernian the previous season, drawing attention to himself by grabbing 5 goals in ten games and in doing so alerting Celtic to his ability and availability. Worthington won the day, and Libbra enjoyed a truly remarkable debut, coming off the bench against Manchester City and scoring a wonderfully executed goal after just 11 seconds, thus entering the Carrow Road record books with the fastest debut goal ever by a Norwich player. He scored again in the following game, a 1-0 win against Wimbledon, swiftly enhancing his newly found status as a cult hero.

UNSURPRISINGLY, therefore, having attained this status and being revered as the man who would solve all of Norwich's goalscoring woes, Libbra didn't score for another 12 games, getting his third of the season in the 3-2 defeat at Crystal Palace on October 28th 2001, and another two in the 2-2 draw at Crewe Alexandra a month later. Libbra didn't score again until March, when he netted in the 1-1 draw at Burnley. A week later, Norwich lost 2-1 at Coventry City, Libbra scoring for the last time. He finished that 2001/02 season with seven goals from 34 league appearances, his final involvement as a non-playing substitute in the first leg of the play-off semi-final against Wolves. His goalscoring record was respectable, given that he only started exactly half of those games. With Iwan Roberts and Paul McVeigh in favour with Worthington, the writing was on *le mur* for Libbra and he was released that summer.

MATTHIEU LOUIS-JEAN

RIGHT-BACK Louis-Jean signed from Nottingham Forest in June 2005. An accomplished player, he had played in nearly 200 games for Forest; the signing seen by many Norwich fans as an exciting one. Sadly, Louis-Jean was injured in his second game, and was eventually released in 2007.

LE JUGE

AS he departed another French player arrived, in the shape of midfielder Julien Brellier, who arrived on a free from Hearts. Brellier came with a big reputation – he had been a terrace idol at Hearts – and there had been talk of him joining Rangers before he joined Norwich. The competitive midfielder failed to create an impression at Carrow Road, making only ten league appearances before he too was judged and ultimately released in early January 2008, his only headline-grabbing performance in that short time being his dismissal against Wolves as Norwich lost their fourth game in seven.

THERE AND GONE

FRENCH defender Jeremy Stinat, on the other hand, made Brellier look like a Norwich veteran. Stinat played in a trial game for Norwich reserves against Wivenhoe in July 2000, before being shipped off back to France the following week.

EARLY CUP STORIES

IN their first two seasons, Norwich entered both the FA and FA Amateur Cups; however, their early performances in both competitions were not impressive. Their first-ever FA Cup match was a preliminary-round clash with Lowestoft Town on September 20th 1902, ending in a 5-0 defeat. Hopes of a better time of it in the FA Amateur Cup were raised when the Citizens, as they were known at the time, beat Lynn Town 5-0 in the first qualifying round. Norwich's cup nemesis, Lowestoft Town were their second qualifying round opponents, this time defeating Norwich 4-2. Norwich ended up playing them four times that season, getting their first victory at the third attempt, the Norfolk and Suffolk League game at Newmarket Road on April 14th 1903, two goals by Collinson securing a 2-0 win. This defeat, their second in the league that season, irked the Trawlerboys. When Norwich travelled down for the return league match the following week (with Collinson absent) they lost 9-2!

SOME FA CUP STATS

NORWICH won their first-ever FA Cup match in the preliminary round of the competition in 1903/04 beating old rivals Lowestoft Town 4-1, that man Collinson again one of the scorers. Their 50th match in the competition was a fifth qualifying round against Folkestone Town on December 1st 1923 (the year of that famous first Wembley final), Norwich edging a close game 3-2. Game number 100 was a first-round Carrow Road encounter against Watford on November 25th 1950, Les Eyre and Roy Hollis scoring the goals in a 2-0 victory. FA Cup match number 200 was another win, this time a 2-1 Carrow Road fourth-round replay success over Tottenham Hotspur on February 1st 1984. Norwich were 2-0 up at half-time, Dennis van Wijk and Mike Channon the scorers and, despite an early second-half effort from Mark Falco for the visitors, Norwich secured the win. In the previous game, a 0-0 draw at White Hart Lane, Norwich legend Mark Bowen made one of his rare appearances for Tottenham, being dropped for the replay; future Newcastle United manager Chris Hughton taking his place. Bowen went on to make 28 FA Cup starts for Norwich, the last coming on January 6th 1995, as the Canaries lost 2-1 at home to Brentford, Bowen being substituted and replaced by Daryl Sutch.

EVER-PRESENTS

DURING their title-winning Division Two winning season of 1985/86, four Norwich players played in every single one of the club's 42 league games; goalkeeper Chris Woods, centre-backs Steve Bruce and Dave Watson, plus midfielder Mike Phelan. Woods and Watson left the club that summer to join Rangers and Everton respectively. Bruce played in all but one of Norwich's games the following season, making his final Norwich appearance in the 2-1 win at Luton on December 5th 1987, before joining Manchester United. His replacement, John O'Neill, signed from Leicester City, was injured on his debut at Wimbledon and never played again. The last of that ever-present title-winning quartet, Mike Phelan remained at the club until the end of the 1988/89 season before joining Bruce at Old Trafford. The Old Trafford hierarchy were clearly influenced in their decision to sign Phelan by his performances for Norwich against them that season; Norwich won both games, the 2-1 win at Old Trafford coming via two goals in the closing minutes, Phelan's own long-range equaliser crowning an excellent performance. Phelan scored one other league goal that season, a 1-0 against QPR on September 10th, the game that saw Andy Townsend make his Norwich debut.

TAYLOR MADE

STRIKER Alan Taylor is 35 years old when he makes his second Norwich debut, at QPR on January 2nd 1989. Taylor, famous for scoring both West Ham United goals in the 1975 FA Cup Final, originally joined the Canaries from the Hammers in 1979 for £90,000, scoring five goals in 24 league games as well as another two in four League Cup appearances. He left the club in the summer of 1980 to play in Canada and after impressing Dave Stringer whilst training at the club, signed again on a monthly contract in time for that game at Loftus Road. Typically, he scores, the goal a result of some frenetic pinball type action in the Hoops penalty area, Taylor getting the last touch of a crazy sequence. He and Norwich are denied a win with Mark Falco equalising in the last few moments. Taylor made a further three league appearances for Norwich that season, all as a substitute and along with Kevin Reeves is one of the few players who have represented Norwich and scored a goal in an FA Cup Final.

PRIOR TO THE PREMIERSHIP

NORWICH'S famous third-place finish in the inaugural Premiership season is one of the club's greatest achievements. Unexpected as it was, the success of that 1992/93 season is rendered all the more extraordinary when their performances of the previous campaign are taken into consideration. Norwich commenced the 1991/92 season with just four wins from their first 15 league fixtures; in addition, £925,000 club record-signing Darren Beckford scored in just one of those games, a 3-1 defeat at Wimbledon on October 5th. This goal doesn't open the floodgates for him and a return of just seven league goals in 30 league appearances doesn't represent good value. Norwich's end-of-season is even more depressing than that poor opening run. Following a 4-3 home win over Everton on March 21st – a game which sees Beckford score a hat-trick – the Canaries lose seven of their last eight fixtures, and end the season in 18th position, just three points separating them from relegated Luton Town, the run including a 4-0 defeat at rock bottom West Ham United.

PREMIERSHIP!

MIKE Walker replaced Dave Stringer for that first Premiership season and selected six of the players who had seen that drab preceding season out with the club for Norwich's daunting opening fixture at Arsenal on August 15th 1992. Striker Mark Robins, bought from Manchester United only days before the opening fixture arrives, is left on the bench. Experienced Nottingham Forest midfielder Gary Megson, later to manage Norwich, was also a new signing who was brought in to provide some bite and experience in midfield. At half-time Norwich were all over the place; 2-0 down, and looking like the favourites for relegation everyone had made them, their miserable run at the end of the preceding campaign continuing. In a stunning 15-minute second-half spell, the game, and Norwich's destiny, isn't just turned on its head but made to perform several backward somersaults. On the hour, with Norwich still 2-0 down, Walker sends Robins on; he makes an impact, quickly scoring, and playing his part as David Phillips and Ruel Fox, dramatically, sensationally, put Norwich ahead. Then, with little over five minutes remaining, Robins chips David Seaman for his second and Norwich's fourth. Game over. Norwich win 4-2, and have the honour of being the very first leaders of the Premiership.

THE YOUNGEST

KRIS Renton is the youngest player to have represented Norwich at 16 years and 276 days. His big moment came when he came off the bench during the Championship game at Leicester City on April 14th 2007. Sadly, injury has subsequently interrupted the young striker's career and he was released by Norwich, following a short loan spell at Brechin City, in January 2010.

DEBUTANT OFF!

WHEN Mark Halsey made his debut for Norwich, at Newcastle United aged just 18 on April 26th 1978, a bright future was expected of the Essex-born midfielder. He will be forever remembered as marking his debut by being sent off. Despite being down to ten men, Norwich drew 2-2 thanks to goals from John Ryan (his 15th of the season) and Kevin Reeves. Halsey didn't feature for the Canaries again until February 27th 1980, a 0-0 Carrow Road draw against Middlesbrough; his third and final game for Norwich followed three days later, another 0-0 draw, this time at Manchester City when he was booked.

THE JARVIS BOY

ANOTHER 'young thing' of whom big things were anticipated at Norwich was Fakenham-born striker Ryan Jarvis. He preceded Kris Renton as Norwich's youngest-ever debutant at 16 years 282 days when he came on as a substitute against Walsall on April 19th 2003 (April seems to be the month that Norwich choose to 'blood' their young players!), his collection of England under-16 and under-17 caps at the time already attracting the attention of bigger clubs. His greatest moment as a Norwich player was on January 3rd 2005 when he scored for Norwich against Liverpool in a Premiership game. Norwich lost 2-1, but Jarvis's goal was special, a curled shot from outside of the penalty area that had Jerzy Dudek scrabbling for air in much the same way Ray Clemence had done, 23 years earlier when another Norwich youth talent, Justin Fashanu, scored an even more spectacular goal. His, as was Jarvis's, also in front of the Barclay End. Like so many young players who explode onto the scene, Jarvis was not able to live up to the expectations club and supporters had of him, and was released by Norwich in 2008.

THE DIY TRANSFER

NORWICH City entered the record books with another 'first' in August 1978 when they signed central defender Phil Hoadley from Leyton Orient. Hoadley's move to Norwich was the first under the new freedom of contract legislation, with a tribunal setting his value at £110,000. His signature was a coup for the Canaries, as they had been up against Everton and Derby County for his services. Hoadley even reportedly turned down an offer from US club New York Cosmos, seemingly preferring to have the likes of John Ryan and Tony Powell as teammates, instead of Franz Beckenbauer. And rightly so. He made his debut for the Canaries in their 3-1 opening-day win against Southampton on August 19th 1978, going on to make 89 appearances for the club. His only goal came in a 4-1 League Cup third-round win over Manchester United on September 26th 1979. Hoadley had been Crystal Palace's youngest-ever debutant, at only 16 years, 112 days, coming on as a substitute against Bolton Wanderers in April 1968.

DID I READ THAT CORRECTLY?

YES, Norwich really did beat Manchester United 4-1 in that League Cup tie (see above). The Canaries had previously beaten Gillingham over two legs in the second round, the 5-3 aggregate win including a goal from ex-West Ham man Alan Taylor in each game. Of added interest to the tie is the fact that the two Gillingham goals scored in Norwich's 4-2 home leg win were scored by Steve Bruce, later to join Norwich. Norwich met Manchester United in the next round, the 4-1 win coming courtesy of goals from Phil Hoadley, Dave Bennett (the skilful winger's first for the club), Justin Fashanu and an own goal from Jimmy Nicholl; Ray Wilkins, with his first-ever United goal, initially put them 1-0 up. Hopes of another good run in the competition were heightened in the fourth round, when, after a 0-0 draw against West Bromwich Albion at The Hawthorns, the Canaries won 3-0 in the replay, Kevin Reeves (2) and Mick McGuire scoring. In the fifth round, Norwich met champions-in-waiting Liverpool, and went down 3-1. As for Manchester United? Norwich met them in cup action again, this time the FA Cup fifth round, in February 1991, winning 2-1 at Carrow Road with Robert Fleck and Dale Gordon scoring in each half.

THE NUMBER EIGHT SHIRT

SEVEN different players wore the number 8 shirt for Norwich during the 1981/82 season. The septet, in selection order, was; Greig Shepherd, Ross Jack, John Fashanu, Paul Haylock, Drazen Muzinic, Dave Bennett, and Martin O'Neill. It was O'Neill who finally made the shirt number his own, debuting with a goal in the 3-2 home defeat to Sheffield Wednesday on February 3rd, and playing in the final 20 league fixtures scoring six goals including the crucial 85th-minute winner at Bolton on March 20th, the 1-0 win being the first of a run of ten wins in 11 games that enabled Norwich to make the last promotion spot.

THE FORGOTTEN MANAGER

MARTIN O'Neill's tenure as Norwich City manager from 1995/96 was so brief it is often unmentioned when his managerial statistics are being discussed, the always accurate (!) national media citing him as starting his career at Wycombe Wanderers before joining Leicester City, Celtic and Aston Villa. The Canaries are one of the five (not four) clubs he has managed, his first game in charge being the club's first game back in Division One (following relegation from the Premiership under Gary Megson) on August 13th 1995, at Luton Town. Norwich won 3-1, two goals from Jon Newsome and a long-range effort from Neil Adams sealing the victory. By November 26th – after a 2-0 win at Watford (Ashley Ward, Keith Scott) – the Canaries were second in the table, just one point behind leaders Millwall. A fortnight later, following a 2-2 Carrow Road draw against Grimsby Town, his name was being linked with the vacancy at Leicester City, following the departure of Brian Little. The following Sunday, he was gone, reportedly resigning after a brief meeting with then chairman Robert Chase, prior to the club's game at – and yes, you couldn't make it up – Leicester City. Keen to show that they could manage without Martin, Norwich raced into a 2-0 lead, Darren Eadie (a future Leicester signing for O'Neill) and Robert Fleck scoring, only to lose 3-2, Iwan Roberts, later to join Norwich, via Wolves, scoring the Leicester equaliser. O'Neill accepted the Leicester job, and Gary Megson returned as manager in time for the next Norwich game, a 1-0 defeat at Portsmouth on December 23rd, making it a not particularly happy Christmas for Norwich supporters.

PLAYER AND MANAGER

NORWICH'S first major trophy success in 1962 was against Rochdale in their second League Cup Final. Rochdale's manager was Tony Collins, who previously played for the Canaries for two seasons from 1953 to 1955.

THANKS ANDY

NORWICH had an ex-player to thank for sealing their Uefa Cup place at the end of the 1992/93 season. Andy Linighan's FA Cup Final winner guaranteed Norwich's place in the competition through finishing third. Linighan, who joined Norwich from Oldham in 1988 for £350,000 had been a mainstay of the 1988/89 side. He appeared in 106 games for Norwich, scoring eight goals, before joining Arsenal for £1.25 million in 1990.

POWELL'S PROGRESS

DEFENDER Tony Powell made an immediate impact at Norwich following his arrival from AFC Bournemouth in August 1974, scoring on his debut as Norwich beat Blackpool 2-1 at Carrow Road. He got another against Millwall on October 5th, but didn't score another league goal for over four years (158 league appearances) when his timely 86th-minute equaliser earned a point in a 2-2 draw at Southampton on November 11th 1978.

FEW GOALS FOR

NORWICH only managed to score 60 league goals in their Division One campaign in 2002/03, 20 fewer than East Anglian rivals Ipswich who finished one point above them in seventh place. A consistent goalscorer for that season might have sealed a play-off place for the Canaries whose leading league goalscorer Paul McVeigh scored just 14, with Iwan Roberts the next best on seven.

GOOD OLD GORDON

IT seems a miracle that winger 'Disco' Dale Gordon ever joined Norwich at all as a youngster, preferring a place at Carrow Road to those offered at Manchester United and West Ham United. Not only that, but, despite being born near Great Yarmouth, he actually supported Ipswich!

GOAL FEAST!

THE goals flew in thick and fast for Norwich shortly into the 1965/66 season when four consecutive league games in September yielded a remarkable total of 24 goals. The entertainment commenced at Derby County on September 4th, Norwich losing 3-1 in front of just over 8,000 supporters. A week later, Norwich faced Southampton at home but shipped in a further four goals, losing 4-3. This defeat saw Norwich slip to 19th place in Division Two, a pending home fixture against eventual champions Manchester City to come. The Canaries redeemed themselves slightly with a 3-3 draw. They had now conceded 16 goals in their opening seven league games and questions were being asked of the City defence, in particular, goalkeeper Kevin Keelan. Any concerns amongst the fans were quickly addressed in the next league game as Norwich won 5-2 away at Bury. In addition, Keelan and his defence suddenly took on admirable miserly qualities, conceding only eight goals in the team's next 13 league matches.

GOALIE OFF!

KEVIN Keelan became the first Norwich City goalkeeper to be sent off when he was dismissed in a league match against Northampton Town on March 20th 1965. Norwich drew the game 1-1 and, with no immediate suspensions in force at the time, Keelan took his place in the Norwich game against Southampton a week later, Norwich losing 1-0. The next Norwich keeper to see red was Bryan Gunn who was sent off twice in his Norwich career! The first time was at Coventry City on April 8th 1988; Gunn getting his marching orders following a heated altercation with the referee regarding his decision to award Coventry a penalty, which had come about after Gunn had brought down fiery Coventry forward David Speedie. Mark Bowen donned the keeper's shirt and gloves for the penalty and remainder of the match, Speedie comically lashing the penalty wide. Norwich still lost though – 2-1. Gunn took an early bath again in the league game at Sheffield United on September 9th 1995, arguing with the referee as the teams left the field at half-time; Gunn, and the entire Norwich team, were angry that a suspiciously offside-looking goal by Nathan Blake had been awarded. Again, Norwich lost 2-1, the winner being headed past stand-in keeper Rob Newman by Carl Veart, Mark Bowen clearly having decided that once was enough.

TERRIBLE THREESOME – CANARIES PLUCKED!

Swindon Town 10 Norwich City 2

HAVING lost their first game of the Southern League season 4-0 at Luton Town on September 2nd 1908, Norwich, given a vote of confidence by manager John Bowman, who picked the same starting XI, travelled to Swindon Town three days later, no doubt determined to make amends. Sadly, things got worse. Trailing 6-1 at half-time, Norwich improved in the second half but the 10-2 defeat remains the clubs biggest-ever loss. Those expecting another goal feast in the return fixture at Newmarket Road on January 2nd were to be disappointed, as the teams fought their way to a 0-0 stalemate. Goalkeeper Peter Roney, who conceded those 14 goals in the two opening matches had retained his place in the side, and was one of seven 'survivors' from the original tie.

Brentford 7 Norwich City 1

IT is surprising to note that the team that would enthral football followers just over a year later by becoming the first Third Division side to reach the FA Cup semi-finals could slip to such an ignominious defeat. It was not even a one-off as the magnificent seven scored by Brentford in that Division Three (South) game on January 11th 1958 had been matched, four weeks earlier, by Southampton who beat the Canaries 7-3. Five of the players who played in the 3-0 FA Cup win over Manchester United in January 1959 also played in the thrashing at Brentford, including goalkeeper Ken Nethercott, plus defenders Ron Ashman and Barry Butler.

Manchester City 6 Norwich City 1

BEATEN Wembley finalists in two of the previous three seasons, Norwich entered the 1975/76 League Cup competition with hopes of yet another run to the final. Their second-round clash against Manchester City provided an early exit from the competition. Following a 1-1 draw at Carrow Road, the replay at Maine Road ended 2-2, Norwich securing the second replay with the second of Ted MacDougall's goals in the 87th minute. The second replay, played at Stamford Bridge, saw Manchester City edge a thrilling, end-to-end contest 6-1, despite Martin Peters swiftly levelling the tie after Dennis Tueart had given the Maine Road outfit a first-minute lead.

TERRIFIC TRIO – CANARIES PLUCKING!

Norwich City 10 Coventry City 2

THE Canaries' record victory came towards the end of an otherwise mundane Division Three (South) campaign on 15th March 1930. Centre forward Thomas Hunt contributed five of the goals as Norwich improved on a 4-0 half-time lead. The sides had also met in that season's FA Cup, Coventry City winning the first-round replay 2-0.

Norwich City 6 Watford 1

NORWICH'S biggest-ever top flight win came with this stroll on April 7th 1984, against a Watford side that included future Liverpool and sometimes England star John Barnes. Robert Rosario, who could never get a mention in the press at the time without a reference to his 'A' level studies being included (such is the scarcity, it seems, of footballers who sit those examinations) made his Norwich debut. The star of the show was John Deehan whose four goals included two penalties. The other Canaries goalscorers were Greg Downs and John Devine, the latter also scored against the Hornets in the Canaries' 3-1 win at Vicarage Road back in October. Norwich finished the season 14th in Division One, ending their season with a creditable 1-1 draw at champions Liverpool, where Devine scored his third league goal of that season.

Colchester United 0 Norwich City 5

NOT many managers can claim a 7-1 and 5-0 victory against the opposing side in the same season. Paul Lambert has done just that. After masterminding Colchester's 7-1 Carrow Road victory over Norwich on the first day of the 2009/10 season – Norwich's first at League One level for nearly half a century – he returned to Colchester with his new club on 16th January 2010 and helped guide the Canaries to a satisfying 5-0 rout. The build-up to the match had been overshadowed by the continuation of legal wrangling between the clubs over Lambert's departure, as well as the Colchester chairman's (I can't remember his name) refusal to give Norwich fans any more than the number of tickets to which they were entitled. The victory was therefore perhaps even more sweet to Norwich and their fans than it might have been. Chris Martin (2), Gary Doherty, Oli Johnson and Grant Holt scored the Norwich goals.

WE ARE WORTHY

NIGEL Worthington was best known in his playing days as the reliable left-back at Sheffield Wednesday. After his first spell in management at Blackpool ended with his resignation, he joined Norwich, working alongside Bryan Hamilton, eventually becoming Canaries manager in 2000 and guiding them to the Division One play-off final in 2002 and promotion as champions two years later. The club's 94 league points in doing so remains a record. His first match in charge of Norwich, initially as caretaker manager, was a 1-0 Carrow Road win over Gillingham on December 9th 2000, Chris Llewellyn scoring.

DOUBLE INTERNATIONAL

ALF Kirchen, who was at Norwich for less than a year before joining Arsenal in March 1935, not only went on to play for England during his time at the Gunners but also had international representation for England at the 1955 Clay Pigeon Championships.

THE ARGENTINIAN

FRANCISCO Gonsalez, native of Vernado Tuerto in Argentina, joined Norwich from Bournemouth in 1930, scoring in only his second game for the club, a 3-1 defeat at Northampton Town on November 1st. He consequently scored in his next two matches as well; a 3-0 home win over Brentford and a 2-1 loss at Crystal Palace. He totalled 19 league and cup appearances, scoring six goals, before joining Newport County. Unusually, he changed his identity for the purposes of playing in English football, abandoning his exotic Latin American name for the more colloquial Frank Peed.

ANOTHER WHO GOT AWAY!

CENTRE-forward Edward Barkas made just one league appearance for Norwich, a 3-1 defeat at Brentford on October 16th 1920. Released by the club, he went on to make over 100 appearances for Huddersfield, winning two league championship medals, as well as an FA Cup runners-up medal. Barkas then joined Birmingham City, where he made over 250 appearances and secured another FA Cup runners-up medal.

STRINGER IN CHARGE

FOLLOWING Ken Brown's dismissal as Norwich manager in November 1987 (accompanied by howls of protest in the national media in support of Brown, a true 'nice guy' of the game), Dave Stringer stepped up, initially as caretaker manager. His first game in charge, at home to Arsenal, sees Norwich lose 4-2, the Gunners scoring their four goals in a 12-minute second-half spell. His first win, a 2-1 success at Luton Town, is the club's first in nine games and following a 1-0 defeat at Wimbledon in their following game, Norwich win the next three, scoring nine goals in the process. The season ended on a low note, Norwich won only one of their last nine league games and finished 14th in Division One. In the 1988/89 season that followed, Stringer put down his marker as one of the best managers the club has had in its history, Norwich finishing fourth in Division One and reaching the FA Cup semi-finals for the first time since Terry Bly and co did, back in 1959. That fourth place finish was all the more remarkable when it is considered that, of their last ten league games, Norwich only got eight points out of a possible 30, a second successive disappointing end to a league season.

STRINGER THE PLAYER

BEFORE joining Norwich in 1963, Dave Stringer played for Arsenal's junior side, as well as having trials with Crystal Palace. He eventually joined Norwich, making his debut on April 10th 1965, slotting in at right-back as Norwich lost 3-0 at Coventry City. He missed the first two games of the following season, but was then a league ever-present, adding five cup appearances to those 40 league games. His first goal for the club was a while in coming, arriving in his 215th game, a 1-1 draw at Huddersfield Town on February 21st 1970. His most famous goal, and moment, for the club was his first-half header in the 1-1 draw against Watford on April 29th 1972, Norwich drawing the game 1-1 and sealing the Division Two title, and promotion, in doing so. In total, Stringer made 497 appearances for Norwich, scoring (after his goal-shy start) 22 goals, the central defensive partnership he formed with Duncan Forbes a mainstay of the Canaries team for many years.

NO DOUBLE FOR BLUES

IPSWICH fans never tire of boring their Norwich counterparts of their one and only league championship success in the 1961/62 campaign. However, any dreams Ipswich might have had of emulating Tottenham's league and cup double triumph the season before were brought to an end in the FA Cup fourth round that same season, Norwich winning a fourth-round replay at Portman Road 2-1, Terry Allcock scoring twice. The replay attracted just 29,796 fans to Portman Road. The original tie at Carrow Road saw a Canaries gate of just under 40,000.

LIVER BIRDS AND CANARIES

THAT 1961/62 league season saw Norwich win the League Cup, as well as knock league champions-in-waiting Ipswich out of the FA Cup. The Canaries' league campaign was disappointing, the club finishing 17th in Division Two. The eventual Division Two champions, Liverpool, had two lively league clashes with Norwich, winning both. Following a 2-1 Reds win at Carrow Road in September, the teams met at Anfield on January 13th 1962, a thrilling match ultimately seeing Liverpool win 5-4, Terry Allcock's feat of becoming one of the few players to score a league hat-trick at Anfield in that defeat the high point.

5-4: THE PREQUEL

NORWICH'S 5-4 league loss at Liverpool in January 1962 came just five weeks after they won a home league game against Middlesbrough by the same score. On December 9th 1961, despite being 2-0 down at half-time, Norwich rallied in the second half. Goals by Terry Allcock, Jimmy Hill, Gerry Mannion and Derrick Lythgoe (2) sealing a dramatic 5-4 win.

JIMMY HILL? SURELY NOT?

YOU'RE right. Norwich's Jimmy Hill was not the Jimmy Hill of *Match of the Day*. The Canaries' Hill was born in Carrickfergus in 1935, joining Norwich in 1958 from Newcastle United for £3,000. Hill, who was capped by Northern Ireland during his time at Carrow Road, scored 66 league goals in 195 league games before joining Everton for £25,000 in 1963.

NEVER SHEARER?

IN February 1989 Norwich manager Dave Stringer realised that if his side was going to maintain its unlikely title challenge some of the responsibility for goal scoring would need to be shared with Robert Fleck. Norwich initially showed an interest in Southampton's Alan Shearer, sending along a scout to watch him play in the Saints home clash with Everton on February 11th; the day that Fleck scored his eighth league goal of the season in a 1-0 Carrow Road success over Derby County. Fleck only managed two more league goals for Norwich that season, ending the season as top scorer and the only Canaries player to hit double figures in the top league, which illustrated the need for a decent striking partner. Shearer failed to score for Southampton that season. However, Dave Stringer clearly knew a good goalscorer when he saw one!

CZECH MATE

NORWICH boss Peter Grant's search for a striker in the summer of 2007 finally ended when the club confirmed the signing of Czech David Strihavka from Banik Ostrava. The 24-year-old checked in at Carrow Road following failed attempts to sign Freddie Eastwood and Billy Sharp. Strihavka had something of a nomadic career in the Czech Republic, playing for five different clubs in six years, including Sparta Prague, a club he represented in the 2004/05 Champions League. His move to Norwich didn't work out and he made just ten league appearances, scoring the one goal in a 1-0 Carrow Road win over Crystal Palace. He was so excited at scoring he was booked for over celebrating!

LATVIA LINKS

PAUL Ashworth's playing career at Norwich City amounted to a spell at the club as a trainee. Despite not making the grade he took up coaching, assisting the Norwich youth coaches. Eventually, he was appointed into similar coaching positions at Cambridge United and Peterborough United, before ending up managing Latvian side FK Ventspils. Ashworth ultimately, albeit temporarily, moved on again, at one point filling in as manager of Russian side Rostov whilst there as sporting director. In doing so, he became the first-ever Englishman to manage a Russian football team.

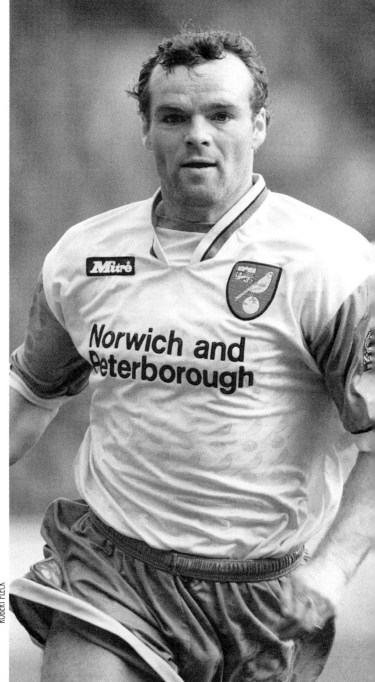

GOALS GRANTED

PRIOR to signing for Norwich in the summer of 2009, striker Grant Holt enjoyed playing spells at Sheffield Wednesday, Rochdale, Nottingham Forest and Shrewsbury Town. He has also spent part of his career playing in Singapore with Sengkang Marine. His move to Forest came after he came to national prominence at Rochdale, scoring an impressive 43 goals in 83 games for a club who were always regarded as perennial strugglers. And, despite being on the bench for much of his time at the City Ground, he still scored 18 goals in the 2006/07 season, ending the campaign being crowned as the supporters' Player of the Season. He then broke Shrewsbury Town's transfer record when they signed him for a reported £175,000 in June 2008, ending the season playing at Wembley in the Division Two play-off final.

YOUTH OF YESTERDAY

NORWICH won the coveted FA Youth Cup for the first, and only time, in the club's history in 1983, beating Everton 6-5 on aggregate over two legs and a replay. The gulf between achievement at that level and transferring it to success in the senior game is aptly illustrated when the 'fate' of the players who represented Norwich in those games is considered. Jeremy Goss is perhaps the best-known player of that side, along with winger Louie Donowa. However, of the remaining nine starters, only left-back Tony Spearing had anything resembling a good career in the game, he ended up making 82 league appearances for the Canaries, including 39 starts in the 1986/87 season.

FARRINGTON IMPRESSES

MARK Farrington was one of the leading lights of the Everton side that Norwich beat in the 1983 FA Youth Cup Final, indeed, as well as scoring four goals over those three games that decided the final, he scored another eight in the competition. When he was released by Everton therefore, Norwich were well aware of his capabilities and signed him at the end of that season. Farrington, like many of his contemporaries in the Norwich side, did not make the step up to senior football and after 18 league appearances and two goals, he moved to Cardiff City and eventually drifted out of the spotlight.

TEN TOP-FLIGHT HAT-TRICK HEROES

Ted MacDougall
Norwich City 5 Aston Villa 3. Division One, 23/08/1975
Norwich City 4 Everton 2. Division One, 06/09/1975
Viv Busby
Norwich City 3 Leicester City 2. Division One, 01/01/1977
Justin Fashanu
Norwich City 5 Stoke City 1. Division One, 16/08/1980
John Deehan
Norwich City 6 Watford 1. Division One, 07/04/1984
Norwich City 3 Watford 2. Division One, 22/09/1984
Darren Beckford
Norwich City 4 Everton 3. Division One, 21/03/1992
Mark Robins
Oldham Athletic 2 Norwich City 3. Premiership, 09/11/1992
Chris Sutton
Norwich City 4 Leeds United 2. Premiership, 14/04/1993
Efan Ekoku
Everton 1 Norwich City 5. Premiership, 25/09/1993

MACDOUGALL'S triple against Aston Villa was the first by a Norwich player in the top flight of English football. John Deehan (vs. Watford) and Efan Ekoku (vs. Everton) both scored four goals in those matches; Ekoku becoming the first player in the Premiership to achieve that distinction. Mark Robins was the first Norwich City player to score a hat-trick in the Premiership, scoring in the 14th, 28th, and 90th minutes in the televised tie at Oldham.

LEAGUE CUP UPSET

FOLLOWING a 2-1 win over Third Division Barnet in the first round, first-leg tie on August 12th 1997, Norwich might reasonably have expected a fairly comfortable confirmation of their progress in the second-leg game at Underhill. When Iwan Roberts put the Canaries 1-0 up just after half-time, and 3-1 on aggregate, it seemed certain to be the case. In just over ten shocking second-half minutes, Barnet scored three without reply to progress 4-3 on aggregate. Norwich experienced similar humiliation in the FA Cup that season, losing 3-0 at Second Division Grimsby Town in the third round.

CANARIES AND SEAGULLS

SEVERAL players have represented both Norwich and Brighton & Hove Albion, otherwise known as the Seagulls. Amongst them are Norwich assistant manager Ian Culverhouse who began his coaching career at Brighton with the club's youth team. Others to have played for both clubs include Mark Barham, Jason Jarrett and Russell Martin.

RIOCH'S IN CHARGE

WHEN Bruce Rioch was appointed Norwich manager in 1998, he became the first person to take up the position who had no previous connections with the club since John Bond had taken the Carrow Road reins a quarter of a century earlier. Rioch was lucky enough to be able to pick a Norwich side that included youth starlets Darren Eadie, Keith O'Neill and Craig Bellamy. All three suffered injury problems during his time at the club and he, like all Norwich fans, can only think of what might have been had all three stayed fit for a prolonged period. Rioch certainly gave youth a chance at Norwich, the epitome of this coming in the 0-0 draw at home to Portsmouth on March 20th 1999, the Canaries finishing the game with seven players aged 20, or under, on the pitch. They were; Che Wilson, Darel Russell, Adrian Forbes, Craig Bellamy, Lee Marshall, Chris Llewellyn and Adrian Coote.

WC BELLAMY

CRAIG Bellamy, uber confident and as cocky as they come, once exasperated his more seasoned Norwich teammates so much that, during one long coach trip to an away game, they locked him in the coach toilet and made the then 17-year-old stay there for almost the whole duration of the four-hour trip.

DEJAN STEFANOVIC

YUGOSLAVIA and Serbia & Montenegro international Stefanovic arrived at Norwich with a good footballing CV in the summer of 2008, his former clubs being Red Star Belgrade, Sheffield Wednesday, Vitesse Arnhem, Portsmouth and Fulham. The only Serbian to have played for Norwich had a very disappointing time in Norfolk; serious injury curtailing the centre-back's season and ultimately his time at the club after 12 league games.

BROWN'S TRIPLE

FORMER Norwich defender Kenny Brown played against Norwich three times in the 1995/96 season, all whilst on loan to three different clubs. On December 30th he played for Reading in their 3-3 draw at Carrow Road then, following another temporary move to Southend, played in their 1-1 draw at home to Norwich on March 2nd. Finally, following another loan move to Crystal Palace, he met Norwich again on the final day, Palace's 1-0 win securing their third-place finish in the table. Brown made 25 league appearances for Norwich, his last game coming a couple of weeks after dad Ken Brown senior left the club, a 1-0 home defeat against Portsmouth. Brown left Norwich for Plymouth Argyle, initially playing under the management of his father again, eventually winning the Pilgrims Player of the Year award in 1990/91, prompting a move to West Ham United, another club with a connection to his father.

CHAMPIONS!

NORWICH'S Division Three (South) winning side of 1933/34 were helped in no small way to their success by the performance of goalkeeper Norman Wharton joined from Sheffield United for £740 in 1931; he played in all of the four league divisions in existence at that time over his career; First, Second, Third (North), and, with Norwich, Third (South).

ENTENTE CORDIAL

NORWICH played their first-ever match against Continental opposition on September 28th 1905, when French side Club Athletique Professionel Parisien travelled to Newmarket Road. Determined to put on a good show for their esteemed visitors, Norwich won 11-0.

THINGS TO COME

NORWICH'S slim hopes of reaching the 2002/03 play-offs came to an end at the City Ground on March 2nd, as Nottingham Forest won 4-0. Norwich were unable to cope with the pace and trickery of Forest's Darren Huckerby. He was one of four Forest players playing who eventually joined Norwich, the others were Darren Ward, Mathieu Louis-Jean and Jim Brennan.

HANSEN'S ROCKET

ALAN Hansen struck lucky in a league match for Liverpool against Norwich on August 30th 1980. His 25-yard shot just before half-time flew past Roger Hansbury and was the opening goal in Liverpool's 4-1 Anfield victory, Dave Bennett scoring a consolation, his first goal for Norwich.

YOU NEED HANDS-BURY

HANSBURY had another torrid time five weeks later when City travelled to Middlesbrough. In front of the *Match of the Day* cameras, John Bond suffered a thousand feathery deaths as his Norwich side were humbled, 6-1, one of the goals being an own goal, via ex-Ipswich man Clive Woods.

BOND'S DELIGHT

A LITTLE over three months after his departure from Norwich, fate decreed that ex-Canaries manager John Bond would have to welcome his old side to Manchester City in an FA Cup fourth-round tie. The game, played on January 24th 1981, saw Clive Baker in the Norwich goal in place of original first-choice Roger Hansbury; however, the Canaries received another thrashing, Bond's new team prevailing 6-0.

THRILLS AT RHYL

NORWICH travelled to non-league Rhyl for an FA Cup second-round tie on December 9th 1950. The part-timers came close to achieving an upset, with only a second-half goal by Noel Kinsey separating the sides. Norwich's reward was a third-round tie at home to Liverpool, which saw the Canaries as underdogs. Norwich upset the formbook winning 3-1, thanks to a Les Eyre goal and two by Tom Doherty.

DEBUT FOR GOSS

JERRY Goss, famous for his European scoring exploits for Mike Walker's Norwich side in the 1993/94 season, actually made his Norwich debut some nine years previously, coming on as a substitute for John Deehan in the Canaries' 2-1 defeat at Coventry City on May 12th 1984.

CAPTAIN MICK

NORWICH paid Coventry City £60,000 for midfielder Mick McGuire in January 1975, the player making his debut in a surprising 2-3 Carrow Road defeat to York City. His first goal came in his fourth appearance, a 3-2 home win over West Bromwich Albion on February 8th, Ted MacDougall scoring the other two. McGuire made 203 league appearances for Norwich in eight years, his final game being an FA Cup sixth-round tie at Brighton on March 12th 1983, coming on as a substitute for Dutchman Denis Van Wijk.

KEELAN'S CAPTAINS

IN Kevin Keelan's near 17-year career with Norwich he played under 19 different captains. In his first game, a 3-1 defeat at Cardiff City on August 24th 1963, the skipper was Barry Butler. Keelan's last-ever competitive game for Norwich was on February 9th 1980, Martin Peters leading the side out for a famous 5-3 defeat against Liverpool. In between those games Keelan played for Norwich sides captained by; Ron Ashman, Phil Kelly, Mal Lucas, Terry Allcock, Freddie Sharp, Laurie Brown, Alan Black, Terry Anderson, Ken Mallender, Duncan Forbes, Dave Stringer, Max Briggs, John Benson (see below), Tony Powell, Colin Suggett and Graham Paddon.

BENSON

DEFENDER John Benson played in 37 league matches for Norwich, captaining the side for one when he replaced the injured Duncan Forbes for the Division Two fixture with Millwall on October 5th 1974. Norwich won the game 2-0 with goals from Ted MacDougall and Tony Powell. Benson rejoined AFC Bournemouth the following January as player-manager.

THE WAR EFFORT

RATHER than shut down during World War I, Norwich City chose to spend the time playing morale-boosting friendlies, mostly against Service sides. During the 1915/16 'season' the club played 39 games, winning 35, losing three and drawing one. Two of the three defeats came against Services teams from Shropshire, the Shropshire Yeomanry winning 1-0 whilst the Shropshire Royal Artillery came away with a 4-1 win at The Nest!

GAMES GALORE

FIXTURE congestion did not prevent Norwich getting promotion in the 1974/75 season. On top of their 42-game league campaign, Norwich played in 15 cup games including 11 in the League Cup, each of their second, third, fourth and fifth round games in the competition needing a replay. The fifth-round ties against Ipswich Town (1-1 at Carrow Road, Norwich won the replay 2-1) came as part of seven games Norwich played in December. In total, the team played 57 competitive matches that season, using 24 players, Ted MacDougall the only City player to start in all of them.

1966 AND ALL THAT

ENGLAND, as we will never be allowed to forget, won the World Cup in 1966, the tournament coming at the end of a distinctly average season for Norwich. The 1965/66 campaign saw the Canaries finish 13th in Division Two, Ron Davies securing all the local headlines with his 18 goals in 40 league appearances. The club did get as far as the FA Cup fifth round, beating Leyton Orient and Walsall to make that stage before losing to Blackburn Rovers 3-2 in a replay at Ewood Park. The first tie, at Carrow Road, had finished 2-2, second-half goals by Davies pulling back a 2-0 deficit at half-time.

BERTIE BIGGINS

IN a nomadic football career that took in eight English league clubs, as well as a spell at Celtic, striker Wayne 'Bertie' Biggins played for one-time Norwich managers John Bond and John Deehan, at Burnley and Wigan Athletic respectively, as well as time spent under former Norwich assistant manager Mel Machin at Manchester City. His spell at Norwich, from 1985 to 1988 saw him work well in tandem with Kevin Drinkell, Biggins often taking the knocks and creating the knock-downs that resulted in many of Drinkell's goals. His Norwich stats of 16 goals from 79 league appearances does not reflect his value to the side at the time, that partnership being one of the major reasons behind Norwich's Division Two title success of 1985/86. One of his best performances of that season came in Norwich's impressive 5-2 win at Sheffield United on March 2nd, Biggins topping off his excellent performance with a last-minute goal.

WAYNE BIGGINS

THE GREAT ESCAPE

FOLLOWING a 2-0 win over West Bromwich Albion on 18th November 1972, Norwich's first-ever season in Division One turned a bit sour as the team failed to win any of their following 19 games. The run eventually came to an end with a 1-0 victory over Chelsea on April 14th 1973, nearly five months later! By now, the club were bottom of the table and clear favourites for relegation. Only two teams went down and Norwich had the same number of points, 28, as the two sides ahead of them, West Bromwich Albion and Crystal Palace. Following that win, Norwich travelled to West Bromwich for a real 'four-pointer', winning 1-0 again; David Cross scoring one of the most vital goals of his Norwich career. The Canaries were now in 20th position and safe. After losing 3-0 at Wolves, in their next game, they were back in relegation danger. As fate would have it, Norwich then welcomed Crystal Palace for their penultimate league game. With a win guaranteeing safety, a season's best attendance of 36,688 had Carrow Road rocking until, half an hour in, a Don Rogers penalty put Palace ahead. Could Norwich respond? Oh yes. Ten minutes before half-time, Colin Suggett scored his first goal for Norwich and, in the dying seconds, Dave Stringer headed home to secure the win and another season of top-flight football.

WINNING NO SPURS

A WEEK after their 1-0 defeat to Tottenham in the 1973 League Cup Final, Norwich swiftly had the opportunity for revenge when the two clubs met at White Hart Lane in a league game. Ron Saunders, eager to focus on getting crucial league points, made three changes to his Wembley team (Briggs, Blair and Anderson out; Hockey, Howard and Mellor in) but it was to no avail, as Tottenham convincingly won 3-0. The first clash between the teams that season was at Carrow Road on October 14th 1972, the Canaries winning 2-1 courtesy of two goals from David Cross, future Norwich player Martin Chivers scoring for Tottenham.

BROWN'S RECORD

KEN Brown holds the record for most matches as Norwich manager, with a total of 367 games at the helm between 1980 and 1987.

HOWARD'S WAY

NORWICH signed striker David Cross from Rochdale for just £40,000 in October 1971, the news being announced over the PA system at Carrow Road during the third-round League Cup match against Carlisle United. Norwich won 4-1, Trevor Howard scoring two of the goals, and scoring them in vain, as it was his place that Cross took when he made his debut on October 9th 1971, in a 1-1 draw at Sunderland. Cross ended that championship-winning season with eight goals, adding another 22 to that total in the 105 league appearances he made for the club, prior to joining Coventry City in November 1973. The previously usurped Howard stuck around, ending up with 19 goals from 156 league appearances, 45 of which were as a substitute.

MR VERSATILE

RICHARD Symonds wore shirt numbers 2 to 11 whilst he was at Norwich, his first appearance in each of the shirts coming in each of the following games, all in the 'old' Division One:

No	Opponent	Location	Date	Result
2	Everton	Away	30/03/79	2-2
3	Manchester City	Away	27/02/79	2-2
4	Wolves	Away	13/10/79	1-0
5	Aston Villa	Away	05/03/83	3-2
			(last Norwich game)	
6	Nottingham Forest	Away	30/04/80	0-2
7	Queens Park Rangers	Away	13/04/79	0-0
8	Liverpool	Away	21/02/79	6-0
9	Chelsea	Away	28/10/78	3-3
			(Norwich debut)	
10	Coventry City	Home	18/11/78	1-0
11	Ipswich Town	Away	26/12/78	1-1

Symonds was a specialist man-marker, and often selected for games where that specific tactic was to be used. In total, he made 68 league appearances for Norwich, five of which were as a substitute, hence completing the outfield set by wearing the number 12 shirt.

IF YOU'RE OLD ENOUGH...

ROSSI Jarvis is the youngest player to have played for Norwich at reserve team level; he was just 14 years old when he played for the reserves against Brentford reserves on February 5th 2003. Later that year, goalkeeper Joe Lewis could have become the youngest player to appear for Norwich in a first-team game. He was on the bench for the Championship game against Burnley on September 13th 2003, acting as cover for Robert Green, aged just 15 at the time. He is also the youngest-ever Norwich City player to be given a first-team squad number (28) during that season. Lewis is the second goalkeeper to have emerged from the Norwich Academy who has been selected for the full England squad, following Robert Green.

GREENO!

GOALKEEPER Robert Green progressed through Norwich's schoolboy, youth, and reserve teams and ultimately into the first team, making his debut against Ipswich Town at Carrow Road in a Championship game on April 11th 1999. He did well, playing a full part in the Canaries' 0-0 draws keeping his place for the game at Tranmere Rovers a week later. That game was drawn 2-2, and, with Andy Marshall restored to the team for that season's remaining matches, Green was back on the bench. He played another five games towards the end of the 2000/01 season and began the following campaign as first-choice goalkeeper. The Canaries' opening fixture, a surprise 4-0 drubbing at Millwall, had the media immediately tipping Nigel Worthington's team for a relegation struggle, but the Canaries rallied remarkably well, winning their next four games, with Green keeping a clean sheet in all of them. The second goalkeeper to have played for England whilst at Norwich (after Chris Woods), he went on to make 241 appearances for the Canaries before joining West Ham United.

WOLVERINE IS A CANARY FAN!

AUSTRALIAN actor Hugh Jackman, famous, amongst other screen roles, as X-Man character 'Wolverine', is a Norwich City fan. Declaring his passion for the Canaries in a Sky Sports interview, he added, "...catching a local derby with Ipswich, that's football at its greatest". It is not known if Wolverine's mutant powers have yet been employed by the Canaries coaching team.

TED UPSETS THE HAMMERS!

STRIKER Ted MacDougall had endured miserable spells at Manchester United and West Ham United before signing for Norwich in December 1973. He managed just five goals in 24 league appearances for the Hammers, and left the club under a cloud, his departure reportedly hastened after a dressing room altercation with 'Mr West Ham', Billy Bonds. MacDougall therefore felt he had something to prove when the clubs met for the first time after his departure, and proved his point, scoring twice at Upton Park on New Year's Day 1974. Sadly for Norwich, they lost the game 4-2, with Graham Paddon, sent the other way as part of the MacDougall deal, scoring twice for the Hammers. MacDougall was happy to bide his time however, and, upon Norwich's return to the First Division in 1975/76, scored the winner on each occasion, as Norwich won both games against the Hammers 1-0. In the game at Upton Park, MacDougall renewed his acquaintance with Billy Bonds, the two of them having another dust up, leading to the always-sporting West Ham followers pelting 'Supermac' with missiles.

YOUNG GLENN

NORWICH games against Tottenham Hotspur are usually entertaining, and the 2-2 draw at White Hart Lane on August 30th 1975 was no exception. The Canaries goalscorers on the day were Ted MacDougall and Phil Boyer and, in amongst all the excitement and MacDougall's 82nd-minute equaliser, people probably took little note of the 17-year-old Tottenham substitute who came on for his debut near the end, a certain Glenn Hoddle.

POOLS BANKER

JOHN Deehan had the unenviable task of taking over as Norwich manager following the departure of Mike Walker to Everton in January 1994. He started his tenure with a seven-game unbeaten league run – all of the games were draws! Norwich's first league victory under Deehan, (you couldn't make this up), was against Everton on March 21st, Mike Walker returning to Carrow Road for the first time. The Canaries duly sent Walker and Everton packing, the 3-0 stroll an excellent result. Defender Ian Culverhouse netted the opening goal, one of only two he scored in a career at the club that spanned 369 games.

RECORD RUN

NORWICH won a club record eleven consecutive home league matches in the 2009/10 season, beating the previous record that had been set by Ken Brown's promotion winning side of 1985/86.

September 29th ....Orient 4-0
October 3rd...........................Bristol Rovers 5-1
October 24th.......................Swindon Town 1-0
November 14th................Tranmere Rovers 2-0
November 24th..Brighton & Hove Albion 4-1
December 5th.................Oldham Athletic 2-0
December 19th............Huddersfield Town 3-0
December 26th............................Millwall 2-0
January 9th...............................Exeter City 3-1
January 23rd..................................Brentford 1-0
January 30th.................. Hartlepool United 2-1

NO CHRISTMAS CHEER HERE

NORWICH took the short trip down the A140 to Portman Road on Boxing Day 1980 full of confidence after the previous game against Coventry City at Carrow Road yielded a solid 2-0 win. Dave Watson, recently signed from Liverpool for £100,000, made his debut in the centre of the Norwich defence, replacing John McDowell. Alas, it wasn't to be a happy debut for Watson, Norwich losing 2-0, goals by Alan Brazil and John Wark securing the Ipswich victory and leaving the Canaries a worrying 19th in Division One.

FROM THE SUPPORTERS

LEFT-half Gerry Howshall signed from West Bromwich Albion in November 1967, the signing due to the efforts of the supporters' club, who announced the move at their annual dinner. However, Howshall failed to scale the heights at Norwich and made just 43 league appearances before moving on to Nuneaton Borough. His capture clearly illustrates how supporters at that time could make a difference, their hard work being responsible for raising the funds needed to sign the player.

UNITED THEY FALL

ON their way to the Division One championship in the 1966/67 season, Manchester United's fans saw little to fear in their fourth-round FA Cup tie against Norwich City at Old Trafford on February 18th 1967. It would seem, therefore, that lessons from that famous match a little over eight years earlier just had not been learnt, as Norwich won 2-1 against a United side that included George Best, Bobby Charlton, Denis Law, Paddy Crerand and Nobby Stiles. Don Heath and Gordon Bolland scored the Norwich goals that shocked the vast majority of the crowd of 63,405. Sadly, Norwich failed to reproduce their cup heroics in the next round, 41,000 cramming into Carrow Road for the visit of Sheffield Wednesday, Norwich losing 3-1.

OHH ARRR CANTONA

ERIC Cantona's full debut for Manchester United was in the clash against Norwich on December 12th 1992 at Old Trafford. In a tight game, leaders Norwich went down 1-0, Mark Hughes scoring before the hour mark.

MR CONSISTENCY

SIGNED from AFC Bournemouth in 1974, a swap deal that saw Trevor Howard head in the opposite direction, defender Tony Powell included 150 consecutive league and cup appearances for Norwich during his time at the club. The run began in a 1-1 draw at Birmingham City on February 28th 1976, finally ending on August 18th 1979; Norwich beating Everton 4-2. Powell made 275 City appearances, scoring five goals, perhaps the most important being in the 2-2 draw against Manchester United in the first leg of the League Cup semi-final in 1975.

NONE FROM THE TOP

THE 1975 League Cup Final between Norwich City and Aston Villa was the first, and still remains, the only time a major domestic cup final has been played at Wembley Stadium between two clubs that were currently playing in top flight football. Interestingly, neither of the other two semi-finalists were from the top division either, Norwich beating Manchester United in their semi, whilst Aston Villa accounted for Chester City.

WAR EFFORT

AS most of Europe tumbled into war throughout 1938 and into 1939, Norwich endured a mediocre season that failed to provide any sort of boost, morale wise, to their supporters. They finished second from bottom in Division Two, thus ensuring that, when regular football resumed again in 1946, the Canaries would be in Division Three (South), the league they had escaped as champions in 1934. One highlight from a dismal season was the 4-0 win over Blackburn Rovers on April 8th 1939, Tim Coleman and Jack Acquroff scoring a brace apiece. Blackburn ended the season as Division Two champions so there was clearly some talent in the Canary ranks, talent that, unfortunately, rarely showed up, as heavy defeats at Sheffield Wednesday (7-0), Blackburn Rovers (6-0), Millwall (6-0), and West Ham United (6-2), all clearly showed. When the Canaries flocked together once more, seven years later, for the start of the 1946/47 season, 17 of the players who had made up the squad for that pre-war season were no longer at the club.

WE LOVE GRANT HOLT!

CENTRE forward and captain Grant Holt scored a total of 30 goals (in all competitions) for Norwich in the 2009/10 season, duly becoming the first player to achieve that distinction since Ron Davies in 1963/64. His first goals were three of the four Norwich scored in a League Cup tie at Yeovil on August 11th 2009, with his first league goals coming in the 5-2 home victory over Wycombe Wanderers eleven days later. By Boxing Day 2006 he had already scored 20 goals, and, had it not been for some unfortunate injuries plus suspensions, Holt would almost certainly have broken Ralph Hunt's club-record 31 league goals from 45 games in the 1955/56 season. He eventually finished with 24 league goals from 39 appearances, capping a memorable debut season by deservedly winning the Barry Butler Memorial Trophy as Norwich City Player of the Season 2009/10.

LUCKY CHARM CULVERHOUSE

FOLLOWING his arrival from Tottenham in 1985, Ian Culverhouse's first 18 league games for Norwich saw the team undefeated. His debut, at Carlisle United on October 12th 1985, saw the Canaries win 4-0, Phelan, Drinkell, Brooke, and Rosario all scoring.

THANKS MCGOVERN

UNFORTUNATELY for Norwich, defender Brian McGovern, signed from Arsenal in August 2000, did not live up to his advance billing as another talented youngster from the Arsene Wenger school of coaching. The 20-year-old made his debut as a second-half substitute in the Canaries' 3-2 defeat at Blackburn Rovers on August 26th, and was in and out of the side throughout the rest of that season. He is, however, remembered by many Norwich fans as the player who scored in the dying moments of the league game at Tranmere Rovers on April 14th, securing a 1-0 win and easing growing relegation fears. It proved to be his only goal for the club, but is certainly up there as one of the more crucial scored by any Norwich player, Norwich having lost five of their previous matches to slip perilously close to the bottom of the Division One table.

PISH PESCH

WHICH Norwich player started his career playing for the Juventus youth team? Paul Peschisolido, the Canadian striker who joined the Canaries on loan from Fulham in March 2001. Peschisolido made five appearances during his loan spell, but failed to worry any opposition goalkeepers during that time. He is one of two Canadian internationals to have played for Norwich, the other being midfielder Jim Brennan.

BUY AND SELL

WELSH international midfielder David Phillips was one of the outstanding players during Norwich's successful Premiership season of 1992/93. He scored many goals whilst he was at the club, including a spectacular overhead kick in the 2-1 win over Crystal Palace on August 29th 1992. Signed from Coventry City in summer 1989, he made his debut on the opening day of the season and scored just three minutes into the Canaries' 2-0 win over Sheffield Wednesday on August 19th 1989. He became a very important member of the team, a player greatly valued by Dave Stringer and Mike Walker, so it came as quite a surprise to Norwich fans when he joined Nottingham Forest for £500,000, the story at the time being that he had been sold to help finance the installation of the undersoil heating system at Carrow Road!

BIG CONTRASTS!

WITHIN a month during the 1993/94 season, Norwich went from playing against Inter Milan at the world famous San Siro stadium, to Adams Park, home of Football League new boys Wycombe Wanderers. Such is the variety in football and what makes it wonderful! The game against Inter Milan, played on December 8th, saw City bow out of the Uefa Cup after a 1-0 defeat. Less than a month later, Norwich, minus recently departed manager Mike Walker, were at Wycombe for an FA Cup third-round match, a tricky game for new boss John Deehan. However, the Canaries played well and won 2-0, thanks to goals from Chris Sutton. Future Norwich boss Martin O'Neill was the man at the helm for Wycombe.

GOAL MUSIC

WHENEVER Norwich score a goal at Carrow Road, the familiar sounds of 'Samba de Janeiro' ring around the ground. The track, by German dance act Bellini, was written in 1997.

HAPPY BIRTHDAY SHAY!

MANCHESTER City goalkeeper Shay Given will want to forget his 29th birthday! He was the Newcastle United goalkeeper on April 20th 2005 when Youssef Safri scored one of the best goals at Carrow Road. Advancing just into the Newcastle half, Safri received a pass from Adam Drury, took one touch, and then powered an unstoppable 35-yard shot into the top left-hand corner of Given's goal. Deserving as it was, the strike wasn't chosen by the BBC as Goal of the Season – it didn't even win the April Goal of the Month!

KEN OF ENGLAND

KEN Nethercott might have beaten Phil Boyer to become the first Norwich City player to be capped by England. Boyer achieved that feat in 1976, but how close did Nethercott come to claiming the honour? He won an England 'B' cap in 1953, and, at a time regular England custodian Gil Merrick was getting some criticism (at one point conceding 16 goals in four England games), Ken must have come mightily close to getting a chance, with perhaps only Norwich's relatively lowly Division Three status holding him back?

DECLAN'S FIRST

GOALKEEPER Declan Rudd became the first Norwich City player to appear at the 'new' Wembley stadium, after it opened in 2007, playing for the England under-16s against their Spanish counterparts on April 28th 2007. Coincidentally, the first English player to score in an official match at the stadium was an ex-Norwich player, David Bentley netting directly from a free kick as the England under-21s drew 3-3 with Italy under-21s on March 24th.

MORE CLUBS THAN...?

STRIKER Trevor Benjamin really has had 'more clubs than Jack Nicklaus', to borrow an old saying of Tommy Doherty's. A professional golfer can have no more than 14 clubs in his bag; Benjamin has gone one better, having had spells with 15 different football league clubs during his career. He had a short loan spell with Norwich in 2002 as a temporary replacement for the injured Iwan Roberts. Benjamin made six appearances but failed to score.

NUMBERS GAME

NORWICH used a total of 34 different players in their relegation season from Division One in the 1973/74 season. Of this total, just two – Kevin Keelan and Dave Stringer – played in all 42 league games whilst one player, Ian Davies, made just a single substitute appearance, the 2-1 defeat at Birmingham City on April 27th. In total, those 34 players made 616 appearances between them. Suggesting that, perhaps, players in a successful side find less reason not to play, Ron Saunders' successful championship-winning squad of just two years earlier, used just 23 different players. Keelan and Stringer, again, ever-presents in the league.

THREE LUNGS

MIDFIELDER Gary Holt, nicknamed 'Three Lungs' in recognition of his amazing fitness levels made 182 appearances for Norwich, scoring just three goals. One was rather special though, as he rattled in a 30-yard screamer at Hillsborough on December 29th 2001, the fifth of the game as Norwich beat Sheffield Wednesday 5-0, a happy return for ex-Owl Nigel Worthington.

INTERNATIONAL MANAGERS

CHAMPIONSHIP-winning Canaries manager Nigel Worthington is now boss of his native Northern Ireland. He is not the only ex-Norwich man to have coached at international level. Former Norwich first-team coach and former player Ian Crook had a spell as manager of American Samoa in 2004.

THREE POINTS FOR A WIN

THREE, rather than two, points for a league win was introduced in the 1981/82 season, and Norwich's first 'three points' were taken in a 1-0 Carrow Road victory over Crystal Palace on September 2nd.

WORLD CUP LOSERS

THE Stoke City side that travelled to Norwich for a Division One fixture on August 30th 1972 featured two players from England's World Cup success six years earlier; Gordon Banks and hat-trick hero Geoff Hurst. Hurst failed to shine and Banks was beaten twice, as Norwich won 2-0, Graham Paddon and Dave Stringer the scorers.

NO MOORE

ENGLAND'S World Cup-winning skipper Bobby Moore made his third and final appearance at Carrow Road when Fulham visited for a Division Two fixture on March 31st 1975. Norwich lost, 2-1, despite taking the lead just before half-time through their own version of Moore – Duncan Forbes. Future Norwich signing Viv Busby played for Fulham in that game.

THAT OTHER 'CITY'

THE Canaries' 2-0 victory over Manchester City on September 9th 1964 was to be the last Canary triumph at Maine Road for a long, long time! A brace by Gordon Bolland secured the points on that day, but it would be 33 years (23 matches!) before Norwich won there again! The curse of Maine Road was finally lifted when the Canaries won 2-1 in a Division One fixture on September 20th 1997, Neil Adams and Adrian Coote scoring, one of the three goals Coote would score for Norwich in 61 appearances.

YELLOW CARD!

THE use of a yellow card by a referee to indicate a player had been booked – or 'cautioned', as it became – was introduced into English football in time for the 1976/77 season. The first Norwich player to see a card matching the colour of his shirt was skipper Duncan Forbes, cautioned in the game at home to Arsenal on August 25th 1976. Ten-man Norwich lost 3-1.

RED CARD!

THE first Norwich player to get a red card was Mark Halsey, dismissed on his City debut against Newcastle on April 26th 1978. The first player from an opposing side to get a red card in a Norwich game was ex-Canary and Brighton defender Andy Rollings, who saw red in the Division One game at the Goldstone Ground on October 27th 1979 for the rather foolhardy act of throwing a punch at Justin Fashanu! Norwich won that game 4-2. Fashanu was the villain a little over a month later when he became the second Canary to get a red card, his early bath at Carrow Road coming during the league game against Aston Villa for a foul on Allan Evans. Just to maintain symmetry, Villa's Denis Mortimer then became the second player to be red carded in a game against Norwich. A feisty game therefore, which ended 1-1, Kevin Bond's 88th-minute penalty securing a late point for Norwich.

A LOAD OF PONY

WHEN Norwich switched kit manufacturers from Mitre to Pony in time for the start of the 1997/98 season, the club had the whole outfit designed by renowned fashion guru Bruce Oldfield in one of the first partnerships of its kind in football. The shirt had a somewhat retro look with its simple navy blue piping and 'Grandad'-type collar, with a further nod to tradition being shown in the new sponsors, world-famous Norwich firm Colmans. The shorts were also slightly different from what had gone before – and what would come again in future kits – the manufacturer's logo and club badge being shown on the side of the shorts, rather than the facing front. As Darren Eadie and supermodel Sarah Thomas modelled the new kits, Oldfield admitted to being initially 'worried' about his creations being covered in mud after a match!

ATTENDANCE DISAPPOINTMENT

NORWICH'S loyal support, both home and away, is the envy of many other clubs in England, with home gates often filling Carrow Road, attendances of nearly 25,000 occurring regularly, even when the club were playing in League One during the 2009/10 season. Nearly two decades earlier, Norwich had started the Division One season (then the top league in English football) with games against champions Arsenal, Liverpool and Manchester United to look forward to at Carrow Road. Attendances had not been as high as the club might have hoped, with Canaries manager Dave Stringer writing in the club's Official Handbook for 1990/91:

"The one thing we have never seemed to do is to increase the number of people coming through the turnstiles. We don't get bad gates – averaging around the 17,000 mark – but it does look as if it is to be fairly static at that figure. I don't think we could have done much more in the way of entertaining football to attract the crowds over the past two seasons and we aim to start again where we left off last year."

STRINGER was proved correct when Norwich played their first game of that season, an entertaining 3-2 win over Sunderland, at Carrow Road on August 25th. The attendance was 17,247. The eventual season average for league games was just 15,527, lower than the figure quoted by Stringer. The lowest league attendance of that season was the 11,550 who rattled around Carrow Road for the game against Coventry City on April 6th. Norwich drew the match 2-2, those fans that did bother to go seeing two ex-Canaries come on as substitutes for Coventry; Kevin Drinkell, and, making his Sky Blues debut, a fortnight after his move from Norwich, Robert Rosario.

SCHOOLBOY DREAMS

THAT 1990/91 season handbook lists 34 young and trainee professionals and associate schoolboys, all registered at Carrow Road for the start of that season. Of that number, only nine made at least one appearance in a first-team game for Norwich City, perhaps the most well known being 'Christopher Sutton', one of the trainee professionals, who went on to play 127 times for the Canaries, scoring 43 goals. Schoolboy Jamie Cureton, then just 15, was with Norwich, now as a 'seasoned professional', at the start of the 2009/10 season, before joining Shrewsbury Town on loan in February 2010.

HEFFER SO UNLUCKY

LEFT-sided midfielder Bob Heffer made just two appearances for Norwich, both during the club's calamitous 1956/57 campaign. His second (and final) game, against Shrewsbury Town on May 1st did see him score as the Canaries won 3-1. His record in the Canaries' reserve side, 24 goals from 54 games, hinted at bigger things to come from the 21-year-old. He moved into non-league circles with Weymouth and never played league football again.

HOSPITAL OPPONENTS

NORWICH faced some high quality opposition in the early years of the Norfolk & Norwich Hospital Cup contests, including Woolwich Arsenal in 1914, the Gunners winning 3-0. In 1954, Manchester United were the opposition, two Alan Woan goals securing a 2-0 win.

DEEHAN FOR GOSS

AN inadvertent elbow from Tony Spearing resulted in his teammate John Deehan requiring attention for a facial injury and led to Spearing's youth team colleague Jerry Goss coming on in Deehan's place, handing Goss his Norwich debut. Goss later recalled: "I ran around a lot and don't think I even touched the ball!"

ANTI CROSS

WHEN ex-Canary David Cross ran out for his new team, Coventry City, in their home league match against Norwich on February 26th 1974, he might have expected some stick from the Norwich fans at the game. However, he might have been more surprised to endure the wrath of his own supporters as well; they were jeering him because of his poor scoring record – Cross hadn't netted for the Sky Blues for nearly two months. Norwich lost 1-0 and it would have been poetic justice had Cross scored the winner. But he didn't. Despite the stick, Cross did well for Coventry, his league record for them of 30 goals from 91 appearances slightly better than his Norwich stats, 21 goals from 84 appearances.

BRYAN GUNN

CUP JITTERS

FOLLOWING the club's embarrassing FA Cup first-round exit against Bedford Town in 1956, many Canary fans would have been nervous at the prospect of facing more non-league opposition at that stage a year later, when Redhill travelled to Carrow Road on November 16th 1957. City fielded six of the side that had lost to Bedford, and got it right this time around, winning 6-1, Ralph Hunt (who also scored against Bedford) getting four of them.

GARY'S GLEE!

WHEN Gary Lineker returned to English football with Spurs, following a spell at Barcelona, his first goal for his new club came against Norwich in the 2-2 draw at Carrow Road on September 23rd 1989. Paul Gascoigne scored the other Spurs goal in an entertaining game that saw Welsh duo David Phillips and Mark Bowen (against his former club) score for Norwich.

TIMOTHY OF SHERWOOD

SIGNED from Watford for £175,000 in 1989, Tim Sherwood's first three matches for Norwich saw him play in three different positions. On his debut, on August 26th, he played at centre-back, as City drew 0-0 with Queens Park Rangers at Carrow Road. He followed that up by coming on for Ian Culverhouse and playing at right-back in the 2-0 win at Manchester United, before reverting to his favoured midfield position during the Canaries' thrilling 4-4 Carrow Road draw against Southampton on September 9th, scoring his first goal for the club. Robert Rosario's 27th-minute equaliser to Paul Rideout's opener was hit on the volley from fully 30 yards, a goal scored in front of the Barclay stand as good as Justin Fashanu's nearly a decade earlier, against Liverpool. Like Fashanu, Rosario's strike earned him the 'Goal of the Season' award, albeit the less prestigious ITV version, awarded by the irritating Saint & Greavsie.

AWAY DAYS

THE Canaries won three and drew one of their opening four away fixtures in Division One in 1989/90, and did so without conceding a goal, the first time a top-flight side had achieved this since Leeds United in 1970.

PARTY POOPER

EX-Canary favourite Keith Bertschin did his best to spoil the Division Two champions' party atmosphere at Carrow Road on April 19 1986, his 65th-minute goal giving visitors Stoke City an unlikely lead in a game Norwich needed to win to wrap up the title. Luckily for Norwich, Dale Gordon equalised ten minutes later, the draw ultimately being enough to confirm Norwich as Division Two champions that season.

OLD FRIENDS

OF all the football league clubs in England, the team that Norwich have played most often is Queens Park Rangers. The two sides have met 111 times in total since their first meeting on January 15th 1910, a 0-0 FA Cup first-round game at Newmarket Road. League encounters between the two sides have been in Division Three (South), League Division Three, League Division Two, League Division One, the FA Premiership and the Championship. The Canaries' best results against their West London opponents have been 5-0 home Division Three (South) wins, both in 1924.

SMITH ON THE BALL

SMITH is the most common surname in the United Kingdom, and reflecting that fact 11 players called 'Smith' have represented Norwich City. The first was Benjamin Smith, a left-back who made 81 appearances for the club between 1920 and 1924. Fast forward to 2009 and the 11th, at present, on that list is Korey Smith. Born nearly one hundred years after Benjamin, Korey was captain of the Norwich Academy side, making his senior debut in a 1-0 Carrow Road defeat to Sheffield Wednesday on April 4th 2009.

SUTTON SENIOR

FATHER of striker and eventual £5 million superstar Chris Sutton, the versatile Michael Sutton, made 46 league appearances for Norwich from 1963 to 1966, scoring three goals; one of those in just his second league appearance, when Norwich lost 6-2 at Middlesbrough on the final day of the 1962/63 season. Chris made his Norwich debut 30 years later, scoring a hat-trick for Norwich in their 4-2 win over Leeds United on April 14th 1993.

MR CONSISTENTS

DURING the Canaries' Division Two campaign of 1960/61, six players appeared in all 42 of the club's league games. The steady six were; Ron Ashman, Barry Butler, Matt Crowe, Sandy Kennon, Bill Punton and Bryan Thurlow. Such consistency helped Norwich to an impressive final placing of fourth in their first season competing at that level, finishing three points behind Liverpool. Butler was an ever-present in the league for all four seasons between 1958/59 and 1961/62, the run making up the majority of 214 consecutive league appearances.

DRURY'S BOW

LEFT-back Adam Drury made his Norwich debut on March 31st 2001, Norwich winning 2-1 against Grimsby Town at Carrow Road. Norwich used 34 different players during that season, of those only Paul McVeigh joined Drury in the squad photo at the beginning of the 2009/10 season, and even he had left the club in the meantime, only to return that summer, via spells at Burnley and Luton Town. Drury therefore commenced the 2009/10 season as Norwich's longest-serving (and by some considerable margin) player, having made over 300 league appearances for the Canaries.

GREAT DANE

WHEN Dave Stringer signed Danish under-21 striker Henrik Mortensen from Belgian side Anderlecht in 1989, the player's pedigree seemed perfect. He had won a championship medal, as well as played in both the European and European Cup Winners' Cups. At £350,000, therefore, he seemed a snip and duly scored on his club debut for the reserves, as well as on his full debut, a 5-0 Carrow Road victory over Brighton & Hove Albion in a Zenith Cup match. He made 12 league appearances that season, failing to score, and only made three, all as a substitute, during the following season, although he did score in a 3-1 home FA Cup fourth-round win over Swindon Town. That was pretty much it for him as a Norwich player as he saw out his time at Carrow Road playing for the reserves (an impressive 25 goals from 54 games), an injury sustained in a game against Ipswich leading to his eventual retirement from the English game at just 23. He did return to Danish football in 1996, winning a Danish Cup winners' medal with Aarhus.

FLEMING'S FAREWELLS

THE last day of the 1993/94 season saw Norwich confirm Oldham Athletic's relegation from the Premiership, Robert Ullathorne scoring for City in a 1-1 draw. Three years later, on the last day of the 1996/97 Division One season, Norwich met Oldham again. This time, however, little rests on the result. The Canaries are marooned in mid-table and Oldham are already relegated, Norwich their last taste of life in Division One before they dropped a league once again. Clearly relaxed this time, the Latics win 3-0 with ex-Norwich man Matthew Rush scoring the second. In both games, the Oldham defence has been marshalled by Craig Fleming; on both occasions, the watching Norwich manager has been Mike Walker. One thing quickly led to another, and, in June 1997, Norwich signed Fleming for £600,000. He comes with a glowing tribute from Manchester United manager Alex Ferguson who had called him "the best man-to-man marker in the country". Fleming's Norwich career lasted until 2007, when he joined Rotherham United. He made a total of 382 appearances, scoring 13 goals, deservedly winning the club's Player of the Year accolade in 2004, despite the arrival and impact made that season by Darren Huckerby.

ELM PARK CLOSES

ANY Norwich fan who went to a game at Elm Park, the former ground of Reading, will tell you of the very basic 'facilities' on offer in the away end at the 102-year-old ground. The last game to be played there was on the final day of the 1997/98 season, against Norwich. The Canaries, minus the recently departed (for a second, and final time) Mike Walker won 1-0, giving caretaker manager John Faulkner a win in his only game at the helm, Craig Bellamy scoring the only goal, as old boy Robert Fleck, now playing for Reading, received generous support from the Norwich faithful.

HONEST BUTLER

WHEN Norwich signed Barry Butler from Sheffield Wednesday in the summer of 1957, club chairman Geoffrey Watling asked his new man what he knew about his new club? With Norwich struggling for cash at the time, Butler's answer matched the economic woes at Carrow Road at that time, his answer to Watling's question being "…only that they are bankrupt"!

WALKER NORWICH RANGER

MIKE Walker's first game in charge at Norwich had been the memorable 4-2 win over Arsenal on the first day of the opening Premiership season in 1992. Following his return for a second stint as Norwich boss, his second 'debut' game at the helm also produced three points, albeit not in quite such a prestigious fixture! Just over 15,000 turned out at Carrow Road on August 17th 1996, as Norwich beat Swindon Town 2-0. Only three players that started the game against Arsenal four years previously made the starting line-up for this game; Bryan Gunn, Rob Newman and John Polston. The Canaries were good value for their win, Andy Johnson and Robert Fleck the scorers. After ten games, it seemed that the old Walker magic has returned to Norwich, the Canaries win 4-1 at Grimsby Town and go to the top of the table, the position maintained with a 3-1 Carrow Road home win over Ipswich Town, Johnson scoring twice, with defender John Polston scoring the other. Unlike their storming Premiership start of 1992, this time Walker and Norwich's bubble did burst! Defeat at Charlton Athletic on November 2nd commenced a run of nine games without a win, and by Christmas, City were mid-table and looking out of contention already, although the relatively giddy peaks of sixth were reached by mid-March to fire talk of a play-off spot. A season that started full of hope fizzled out and Norwich finished in 13th position, eight points short of that elusive play-off place.

21ST CENTURY CANARIES

NORWICH'S first match of the 21st century was a home league match against Portsmouth on January 3rd 2000. Craig Fleming has the honour of scoring the club's first goal of the new millennium after nine minutes, Iwan Roberts securing a 2-1 victory from the penalty spot.

GOOD HUNT-ING

PERCY Varco's record of 29 league goals in a season, set in 1928, stood for 28 years; the man who finally broken it was Ralph Hunt, who netted 31 times from 45 league appearances during the 1955/56 season. He also scored 2 FA Cup goals in three matches. Up to the beginning of the 2010/2011 season, Hunt's league total was still a record for a Norwich City player.

ROYAL APPOINTMENT

SIGNED from Bristol City for £90,000 in 1980, ex-England centre forward Joe Royle made 47 appearances for Norwich, scoring ten goals. All but two of those appearances came in the 1980/81 season, one of his goals coming in an impressive 2-0 win for Norwich at his old club Everton, on April 11th.

LAWRO'S SHAME

NEVER short of an opinion on BBC's *Match of the Day* programme, pundit Mark Lawrenson would probably prefer not to analyse his performance in Liverpool's game at home to Norwich on April 23rd 1983. A Liverpool side including the likes of Hansen, Dalglish and Souness lost 2-0, Lawrenson scoring the first, a header past his own keeper, Grobbelaar.

OPPOSING STRIKE FORCE

TWO members of the Canaries' promotion-winning squad of 2003/04 teamed up to play against Norwich on November 23rd 2000, Crystal Palace's Leon McKenzie and Mattias Svensson causing the City defence no end of problems with, agonisingly, Svensson scoring the only goal in the 90th minute as Norwich went down to their first defeat in nine games.

GOALS FIRST

THE first Norwich player to score over 25 league goals in a single season was Percy Varco, whose total for the 1927/28 season was 29 goals from 41 league games. He scored two in a game on seven separate occasions.

DRAW SPECIALISTS

NORWICH are often seen as draw specialists, a fact beautifully illustrated by the Football League record they set in the 1978/79 season. The Canaries drew 23 of their 42 league games; turning just 12 of those draws into wins would have seen City finish runners-up to Liverpool! The club drew a further 14 games in the following season, including a 3-3 Carrow Road epic against Ipswich Town on Boxing Day 1979, Keith Robson's 89th-minute goal securing the point and sending hordes of Ipswich fans home very unhappy!

AWAY DAY BLUES

NORWICH lost 21 consecutive away league games between September 13th 1930 and September 9th 1931. During that run, the Canaries scored nine goals but conceded 56, including seven at Walsall and five at Swindon Town. The inglorious run finally came to an end on September 19th 1931, with a 3-1 victory at Clapton Orient.

THREE MANAGERS

WHEN the Canaries met Notts County at Meadow Lane in a Division One fixture on November 12th 1983, three of the County players starting on that day went onto have spells as manager of Norwich City; Martin O'Neill, Nigel Worthington and Glenn Roeder. The game ended 1-1, Mark Barham scoring for Norwich only for ex-City favourite Justin Fashanu to equalise shortly afterwards.

O'NEILL THE PLAYER

AMONGST all of the debate about Martin O'Neill's short spell as Norwich manager, it is often forgotten that he had two productive playing spells at the club. He initially signed – to the great surprise of many Canaries fans – from Nottingham Forest in February 1981, the ease of his capture, and seemingly very low price (£250,000), being put down to the fact that the intelligent and opinionated O'Neill and his outgoing manager at Forest, one Brian Clough, could no longer see eye-to-eye so one had to go! O'Neill's canniness was reflected in the fact that he insisted on a release clause in his contract being activated if the Canaries were relegated. Unfortunately for Norwich, they did go down at the end of that season, and O'Neill left for Manchester City, Norwich making a swift £25,000 profit on the deal. However, O'Neill and Manchester City were not a match made in heaven, but it seems O'Neill and Norwich City were, and almost a year since he was first signed the talented Irish midfielder was back at Carrow Road, playing a full part in ensuring the Canaries made an immediate return to Division One at the end of that season. In total, O'Neill made 75 appearances for Norwich, scoring 13 goals, the last of which came in a famous 2-0 win at champions-elect Liverpool on April 23rd 1983; his last Canaries game was on the final day of that season, a 2-1 Carrow Road victory over Brighton & Hove Albion.

SO LONG, LOL...

FOLLOWING a heavy 5-2 defeat at Portsmouth on April 12th 1969, Norwich fans were expecting a morale boosting return to form in the next game, the penultimate Carrow Road fixture of the season against champions Derby County. Norwich had won the same fixture the previous season, 3-2, with Hugh Curran one of the scorers; Brian Clough's first game at Carrow Road as a manager. Just over 18 months on and Derby are a different side, their season had seen them go 22 games without defeat, whilst Curran, the Canaries 'big name' had left the club. The game, therefore, pretty much went to form, Derby won 4-1 and with that result, City manager Lol Morgan is 'asked' to resign. This turns out to be a turning point in the club's history as in June the club appoint Oxford United's manager Ron Saunders as Morgan's successor.

SAUNDERS STARTS

RON Saunders has etched himself a permanent place in Canaries folklore for being the man who led them to the top division of English football for the very first time in 1972. His first season in charge, 1969/70, did little to suggest of the heady times coming to the Norfolk footballing public. Norwich won just five of their first 14 league fixtures and lost four games on the bounce at one point in the autumn, as well as exiting both cup competitions at the first hurdle. However, as the season entered its final quarter, Saunders' fit and organised side went on an impressive end-of-campaign run and were undefeated in their final 12 league games, a sequence that included a 6-0 home victory over Birmingham City on April 15th 1970, the first time Norwich had scored that many goals in a league game since 1963. The Canaries finished Saunders' inaugural season in 11th spot, only two places higher than the 13th position that had seen Lol Morgan sacked a year earlier, but with the undefeated run of games at the end of the season, as well as the performances of a more resolute defence. City conceded ten fewer league goals over their 42 league games which did much to suggest that there was a change in the air. The Canaries' top goalscorer that season was Ken Foggo, whose record was 11 goals from 43 league and cup games.

HAPPY NEW YEAR!

NORWICH have had varying degrees of success during New Year's encounters when league football has been played on New Year's Day. In 1977, a Viv Busby hat-trick secured a 3-2 win over Leicester City, Norwich's third league win in a row. Two years later, John Bond demanded that the league match at Crystal Palace be postponed, due to the icy conditions on the pitch. His appeal is noted, turned down, and a delicate 0-0 ensues, with both sides focused on keeping their feet and avoiding injury. No such worries in 1949, as Exeter City are soundly beaten 3-0 at Carrow Road, Len Dutton one of the scorers in his first appearance of the season. New Year joy was not so evident in 1990 as Norwich lost 1-0 at home to Wimbledon, a last-minute goal by Terry Gibson ruining the Carrow Road bonhomie.

SNOW STOPS PLAY

THE winter of 1962/63 was one of the coldest in history throughout Great Britain, and it certainly played havoc with the nation's sporting fixtures. Following a narrow 4-3 Carrow Road defeat to Middlesbrough on December 29th, it's three weeks before City play again, convincingly winning 3-0 at Bury on January 19th. Terry Allcock shrugged off the freezing temperatures with a hat-trick. However, the snow and ice then sets in, and even the resolute Allcock cannot come out and play. City had no games for over a month, a 4-2 home win over Rotherham United being their first match since the 'big freeze' and that coming on February 23rd! It's business as usual for Allcock who bags another two goals. Such was the fixture backlog caused by the weather at that time, City ended up playing nine games in March 1963, five of which were FA Cup matches. The season eventually ends on May 21st, and it's another goal feast at Middlesbrough, City losing again this time 6-2.

FA CUP DISTRESS

BETWEEN 1969 and 1975, Norwich went out of the FA Cup at the third-round stage on every single occasion, scoring just four goals but conceding 23 during that woeful run. Pick of the bunch was a 5-1 demolition at Wolverhampton in 1971, Ken Foggo netting the solitary Norwich goal.

DICKSON OF YELLOW AND GREEN

POWERFUL midfielder Dickson Etuhu joined Norwich from Preston North End for a reported fee of £450,000 in early 2006. He had, prior to signing, completed a two-month loan period at Carrow Road making his debut in a 2-0 home win over Luton Town on November 19th 2005. His first goal came in a League Cup victory over Torquay United the following August. Since leaving Norwich – his departure activated by a controversial release clause that had been included in his contract – Etuhu has been sold for over £1 million on two occasions; Norwich receiving £1.5 million for him from Sunderland in July 2007, with Fulham paying the same amount to lure him away from the Black Cats just over a year later.

WHAT MIGHT HAVE BEEN?

THE Canaries' famous 2-0 home win over arch-rivals Ipswich Town in the second leg of the 1985 League Cup semi-final has gone down in club folklore, Steve Bruce's towering header in the dying moments adding a certain "you couldn't make it up" feel to the occasion, that goal sealing Norwich's place at Wembley. Bruce, in his first season at the club, had already made his mark, scoring an own goal in the 3-3 home draw against Liverpool on the first day of the season. However, it was a disallowed goal that perhaps made the biggest impact on that League Cup semi-final. Ipswich had won the first leg at Portman Road 1-0, Mitch D'Avray scoring after just six minutes. The seminal moment was a controversially disallowed second goal for the Suffolk club, Dutch midfielder Romeo Zondervan scoring. To his disbelief, referee Don Hutchinson, who had run the line in the 1981 FA Cup Final, decreed that the ball had not crossed the line, and the embattled Canaries lived to fight another day.

CITY STOP REDS RUN

NORWICH'S 1-0 League Cup Final win over Sunderland in 1985 had, finally, brought to an end four consecutive successes in the tournament for Liverpool from 1981 to 1984. David Fairclough, who failed to make the Canaries XI on the day of the final, had played in the 1983 final for Liverpool as a late substitute in their victory over Manchester United.

WELSH DRAGONS

WELSH international strikers Iwan Roberts and Craig Bellamy formed a lethal strike partnership in the 1998/99 season netting 22 times between them in Norwich's opening 21 league games. The duo's run was broken in controversial circumstances in the next game, a 2-2 draw at Wolves on November 14th. Roberts duly scored against his former club to take his total for the season to ten, but Bellamy's run of goals was temporarily ended when a tackle from Kevin Muscat required ten stitches. Muscat was not even booked for the foul, but Bellamy's momentum was gone and he scored only four more league goals that season. The Roberts-Bellamy partnership is often neglected when fans talk of the great Norwich forward lines, but had Bellamy's season not been interrupted, the two of them may well have helped fire Norwich into a play-off spot.

RAM RAID

DERBY County shocked the Carrow Road crowd of just over 25,000 in the team's Division One fixture on February 23rd 1973, taking a 3-0 lead in less than 20 minutes. Trevor Howard and Dave Stringer brought the score back to 3-2 but the Canaries could not complete a comeback; and Jeff Bourne's second sealed a 4-2 win. Future Canaries manager Bruce Rioch played for Derby on the day, his team's win dumping Norwich to the foot of the table.

RIOCH AYE THE NOO?

BRUCE Rioch, Norwich manager from 1998 to 2000, was Scotland's captain in the 1978 World Cup finals, but those who have him down as one of the nine Scottish managers the Canaries have had in their history (up to, and including Paul Lambert) would be wrong, for Rioch was born in Aldershot, part of that quintessentially English county, Hampshire.

BERNARD'S FAREWELL

BERNARD Robinson's 380th and final game for Norwich could hardly have been scripted better by Steven Spielberg. The wing-half made his exit in a 2-0 Carrow Road win over Ipswich Town on March 12th 1949, a crowd of over 35,000 there to witness the occasion.

HUNT HAUNTS NORWICH

STRIKER Andy Hunt had an unsuccessful trial with the Canaries in 1990, eventually going on to play at non-league level with Kettering Town. By the time Norwich played Charlton Athletic at Carrow Road on January 2nd 2000, he had worked his way back into the professional game and was determined to show the club who had rejected him a thing or two. He did so in some style, scoring a hat-trick as Charlton Athletic convincingly won 3-0.

ALLCOCK'S MENTOR

CANARIES Hall of Fame member and club-record FA Cup goalscorer Terry Allcock was something of a 'wise old head' to the younger players in the Norwich ranks as he neared the end of his career at the club, teenage striker Trevor Howard, who played alongside Allcock as he played his final games at the end of the 1968/69 season being one of them. Allcock himself had learnt his goalscoring trade as a teenager at Bolton Wanderers, one of the players who he looked up to during his early years in the game there being none other than one of the most prolific English goalscorers ever, Nat Lofthouse.

HAMILTON'S NEW BOYS

IN the final eight games of the 1999/2000 season Norwich manager Bryan Hamilton handed debuts to six players. The sextet in question were; Des Hamilton (no relation), Garry Brady, Raymond De Waard, Gaetano Giallanza, Fernando Derveld and Paul McVeigh. Of that six, only McVeigh proved himself to be anything like a good signing, becoming part of Nigel Worthington's Championship-winning squad of 2003/04. Hamilton and Brady had come in on loan and were not retained whilst Giallanza's career was ended by injury. Dutchmen De Waard and Derveld were swiftly released by Worthington soon after he became manager in 2001.

WORTHY THE SPOILER

NORWICH were top of the Premiership when they travelled to Hillsborough to play Sheffield Wednesday on January 10th 1993. A goal by future Norwich manager Nigel Worthington won the points for the Owls, as the Canaries slipped to third.

GUNN THE GER?

LEGENDARY Norwich goalkeeper Bryan Gunn nearly ended up not coming to Carrow Road at all! As it became clear that he was not going to dislodge Jim Leighton as Aberdeen's first-choice keeper, a move looked more and more likely with at one point Walter Smith looking odds-on to take him to Glasgow Rangers. Before anything came of the proposed move, Smith was gone and Graeme Souness had taken over at Ibrox Park signing the then Norwich goalie Chris Woods instead. Gunn therefore ended up replacing the man who had denied him that move, heading south to Norwich to replace Woods and making his Canaries debut in the 2-1 win over Tottenham at Carrow Road on November 8th 1986. The game is also notable for the fact that Ian Crook scored his first goal for Norwich in that game against his former club.

MALKY MAKES HIS MARK

NORWICH signed centre-half Malky Mackay in September 1998, a bargain at just £350,000 from Celtic. Mackay made his full debut in the 2-0 home win over Birmingham City on September 26th, commencing a famous and successful partnership with Craig Fleming in that game. His first goal for the Canaries came just three days later, in a 2-2 draw at home to Sunderland. Malky made a total of 232 appearances for Norwich scoring 17 goals, as well as making his international debut for Scotland. As Watford manager, Mackay brought Arsenal youngster Henri Lansbury to Vicarage Road on loan in August 2009, the youngster having been known to Mackay during his brief time at Carrow Road as a schoolboy in 1999.

NO NO NORWAY...

ENGLAND fans will not easily forget the team's surprising, some would say embarrassing, defeat in a World Cup qualifying game against Norway in September 1981, the Norwegians' 2-1 win in Ullevaal prompting the famous "your boys took a hell of a beating" from the home television commentator Bjorge Lillelien. Amongst the victorious Norway team on that day was Arne Larsen Økland. Just under 18 months before his and Norway's finest hour, Økland had a trial spell at Norwich but, after a week spent at Carrow Road, Norwich manager John Bond decided against signing him.

OOH HUCKERBY!

IT is likely that no footballer, certainly in modern times, has made quite as a dramatic and long-lasting impact on Norwich City than Darren Huckerby. Originally signed on loan by Nigel Worthington to give a bit of attacking flair to what had been a stuttering start to the 2003/04 season, Huckerby made his debut in the home game against Burnley on September 13th going on to make a total of 203 appearances for the Canaries, scoring 48 goals. His influence on the team and the hero worship he swiftly acquired from the spectators was almost instantaneous as he created the second goal for Iwan Roberts in that Burnley game, Norwich winning 2-0. His first goal came in his third start, a 1-1 draw at Stoke City. This was swiftly followed by his first goal at Carrow Road, a trademark run from the left ending in him being upended in the penalty area, Huckerby putting away the resultant spot kick with some panache. He scored five goals in his 16-game loan period at Norwich, the last coming in a superb team performance on December 13th 2003 as Norwich beat Cardiff City 4-1. The scenes at the end of the game, with Huckerby being given a Norwich shirt by a supporter, and applauding the fans as he left the pitch seemed final; the club were interested in signing him permanently but both Huckerby's 'parent club', Manchester City, and the player's agent seemed insurmountable obstacles, the latter stating that Huckerby was a "Premiership player with Premiership aspirations and Premiership wage demands". However, after much debate between club and player, Huckerby signed for Norwich on a permanent basis for just £750,000 on December 26th – a Boxing Day bargain buy if ever there was one. He made his 'second debut' in the club's third round FA Cup defeat at Everton on January 3rd 2004. Ironically, given that his first goal for Norwich at Carrow Road had been against Crystal Palace, he also scored the first goal of the club's subsequent Premiership campaign, again, at Carrow Road and against Crystal Palace. Despite relegation that season, and being linked with moves to Liverpool and Celtic, Huckerby remained loyal to Norwich, his last game and goal for the club coming on May 4th 2008, Norwich losing 4-1 at Sheffield Wednesday. Two days later the club announced that he was not being offered a new contract for the following season, bringing the curtain down on a sparkling five-year spell. Huckerby is now a matchday host at Norwich.

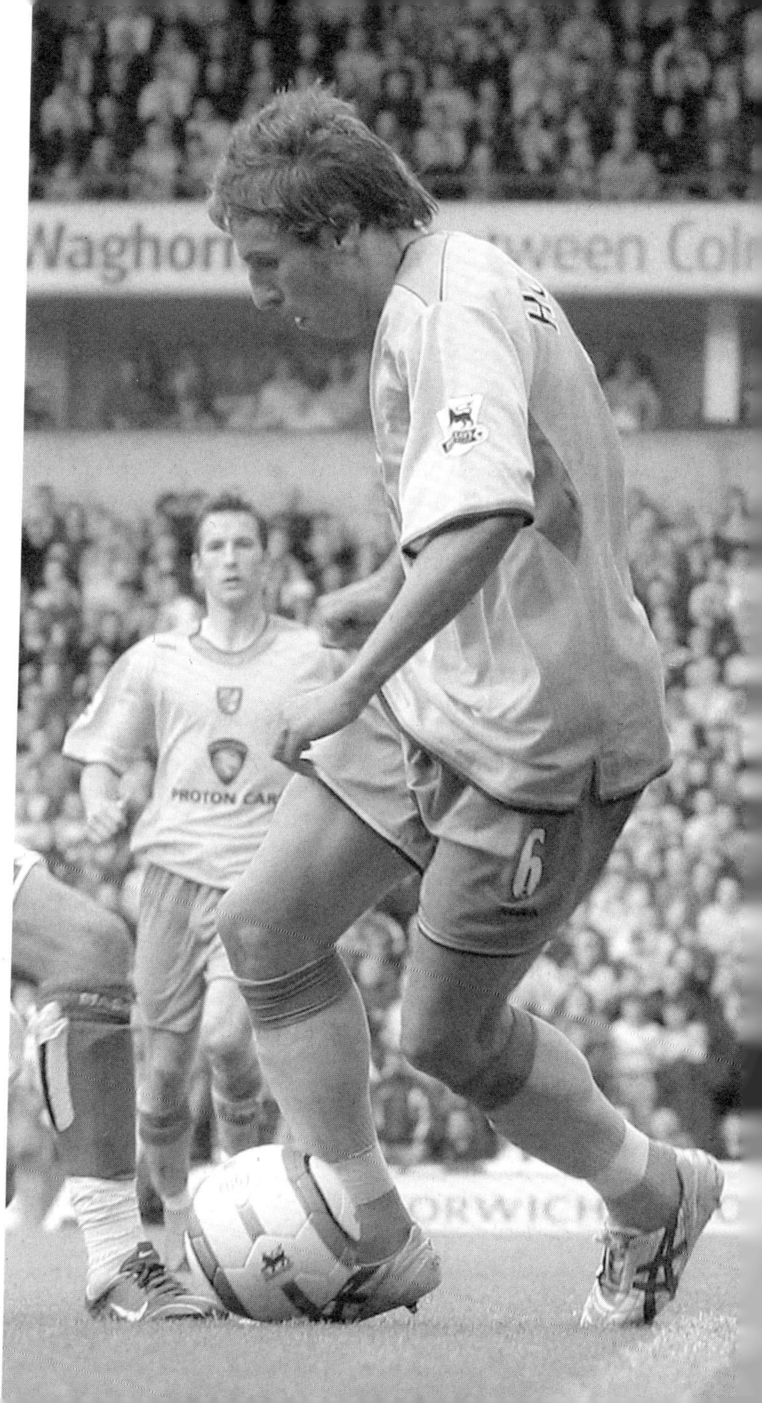

DARREN HUCKERBY

TEN-MINUTE BLITZ

NORWICH looked set for a valuable point in their game at Birmingham City on 20th February 1981, an unremarkable game entering its last fifteen minutes at 0-0. However, something then stirred in the Birmingham team, and they rapped home four goals in ten minutes, swiftly turning a crucial point into a 4-0 hiding. Kevin Bond, playing in what would be his last game for the Canaries' missed a first half penalty. The slaughter at St Andrew's turned out to be goalkeeper Roger Hansbury's penultimate game for the Canaries, his last appearance for the club came a week later as Norwich broke a run of six successive league defeats, beating Brighton 3-1, a game that saw Martin O'Neill make his Norwich debut. By the time of the Canaries' next fixture, a 3-0 loss at Wolves, Chris Woods had arrived from Queens Park Rangers on loan and made the number 1 spot his for the next five years.

SWEET REVENGE

THE Canaries had more than that 4-0 defeat at Birmingham in mind when the two sides met at Carrow Road in their first league clash since that loss. Adding spice to the proceedings, was the presence of a certain ex-Norwich manager, Ron Saunders, now in charge at St Andrew's, returning to Norwich for the first time as Birmingham manager; but he failed to rouse his new charges, as Norwich won 5-1. Norwich striker Keith Bertschin particularly enjoyed himself, scoring two against his former club; Martin O'Neill, with two goals in four minutes, and Mark Barham completing the rout. To prove the result was no fluke, City travelled to St Andrew's for the return fixture on 9th April 1983, and hit four without reply, Bertschin grabbing another brace, with John Deehan helping himself to two more.

DIXIE AND BERTSCH

NORWICH secured Division One safety at the end of the 1982/83 season with an impressive run-in that saw them win six, and draw three, of their last ten league fixtures. Pivotal to the team's success that season had been the goalscoring form of strike duo Keith Bertschin and John Deehan, who ended with 28 league goals between them, out of the team's season-end total of 52.

TWO REDS

TWO Norwich players received red cards in the 2-0 loss at Tranmere Rovers on October 4th 1997; Rob Newman and Mike Milligan.

ASA'S RECORD

WHEN Asa Hartford lined up for Norwich in the 1985 League Cup Final against Sunderland, he became the first player to appear in three League Cup finals with three different clubs. His first had been in 1970 when he played for West Bromwich Albion, aged just 19, in their 2-1 defeat to Manchester City. One of his Baggies teammates on the day was Colin Suggett, who later joined Norwich. In 1976, Hartford reached the League Cup Final again, as a member of the Manchester City side that defeated Newcastle United; the City side on the day featuring another three players who would go on to represent the Canaries: Joe Corrigan, Willie Donachie and Joe Royle.

OLD TIME WISDOM

THE 1925 edition of the Norwich City Supporters' Club handbook featured a quote that is perhaps even more applicable in these times when the demands of Canaries fans are so high; "Come and be a supporter not a spectator, the latter pays and expects, but a supporter pays and hopes."

THE FIRST LOAN

THE first player that Norwich brought in on a loan basis was Crystal Palace centre-half Bobby Bell, who joined for one month in February 1972, playing three games. Unfortunately for Bell, the last of those three matches was a 4-0 defeat at Birmingham City.

NEARLY MEN

NORWICH came close to winning the Division Three (South) title in the 1951/52 season, missing out by only five points. Plymouth Argyle ended the season as champions, but not before Norwich beat them 3-0 in the penultimate game, with Ron Ashman scoring twice. The fixture at Home Park had seen Plymouth win 3-1.

EFAN AND HELL

FOLLOWING his £900,000 departure to Wimbledon in October 1994, it didn't take Efan Ekoku long to open his account for his new club. Just over an hour had elapsed at Selhurst Park when he scored for the Dons in their game against Norwich! It was the Canaries' sixth defeat in a row in the fixture. The previous season had seen them lose 3-1, with Ekoku scoring for Norwich!

RED HOT ASH

NORWICH signed Ashley Ward from Crewe Alexandra to replace Wimbledon-bound Efan Ekoku, and the new boy didn't take long to make an impact, scoring two first-half goals to put the Canaries 2-0 up at home to Chelsea. Jamie Cureton scored a third, giving Norwich an impressive win in a season that was destined to go to the wire.

SO NEAR

NORWICH needed to win their penultimate league game at Leeds United on May 6th 1995 to have a chance of avoiding relegation. They were 1-0 up at half-time, thanks to an Ashley Ward goal. Leeds equalised with a penalty, then, in the dying seconds, Carlton Palmer popped up to give them victory confirming relegation from the Premiership. Had Norwich hung onto their lead, they would have stayed up at the expense of Crystal Palace.

VASPER'S PLIGHT

GOALKEEPER Peter Vasper had the unenviable task of arriving at Norwich just as club legend Kevin Keelan was well and truly embedding himself into the team. Vasper joined from non-league Guildford City in 1968 and following an injury to Keelan, played in 12 consecutive league games towards the end of the 1967/68 season, only to see Keelan step back into the side for the last-day clash against Cardiff City. Almost exactly the same thing happened again the following campaign – with Keelan injured again, Vasper appeared in a further ten league games with Keelan again making his return on the last day of the season. Vasper played in just nine more league games, plus an FA Cup third-round defeat against Wrexham for Norwich, before leaving for Cambridge United in September 1970.

WALFORD'S WANDERINGS

STEVE Walford has accompanied Martin O'Neill at all five of his managerial positions in English football, beginning at Wycombe, the brief period at Norwich, before moving onto Leicester City, Celtic and Aston Villa. Like O'Neill, Walford spent part of his playing career at Norwich, joining from Arsenal for £175,000 in March 1981. It would have been at that time that he and O'Neill commenced their friendship which ultimately led to them working together at a managerial level, the two teaming up for the very first time in the Canaries' Division One game at Wolverhampton Wanderers on March 14th, a game Norwich lost 3-0. O'Neill had only arrived at the club himself a fortnight before Walford, and was immediately made captain by Ken Brown; the two new arrivals did their level best to help Norwich avoid relegation, but sadly, to no avail. When O'Neill rejoined Norwich after a brief spell at Manchester City, Walford had established himself in the Canaries team, and the pair renewed acquaintances. Walford made a total of 108 appearances for Norwich, scoring two goals, before leaving to join West Ham United in August 1983 for £160,000. He teamed up again with O'Neill when he joined Wycombe Wanderers in 1989, and their working relationship has endured ever since.

FROM NORWICH TO AJAX!

DUTCH right-back Jurgen Colin struggled to establish himself at Norwich following his arrival at the club from PSV Eindhoven in 2005. His signing was certainly seen as something of a 'steal' for Nigel Worthington, given that Premiership Everton had also, reportedly, been interested in signing him. He made his debut in the 1-1 Championship clash against Crystal Palace on August 13th, but was never quite able to display either the confidence or forward-going mobility that had prompted his arrival. At one point, he lost his place at right-back to Craig Fleming, a player moved out of position to replace him with Fleming long-established at Norwich as a centre-back. In a stop-start two-year spell at Carrow Road, Colin made 64 appearances for Norwich, before moving back to Holland, and Ajax Amsterdam in July 2007. He is perhaps the only Norwich player who has left a club that has won the European Cup in order to join Norwich, only to ultimately leave Norwich to join another that has also won Europe's premier football trophy!

SOD'S LAW OF CARROW ROAD

THE 2008/09 Championship season ended with relegation to League One meaning that the Canaries would be playing in the 'old' Third Division the following season – for the first time since 1960. One of the few highlights of the season had been the clash with eventual champions Wolves on October 21st. Norwich went into the game on the back of three consecutive defeats, scoring only one goal in the process, whereas Wolves were top having won eight of their first 11 fixtures. With Norwich having won only two games themselves, it was more hope than expectation that surrounded Carrow Road that evening, the game was the proverbial 'away banker'. So what happened? Well, Norwich won, of course. Leroy Lita, on loan from Reading, scored a hat-trick as the leaders were humbled, 5-2. But maybe no-one should have been that surprised? Sods Law of Carrow Road states that, "*...however well we are playing, and however winnable a game might seem, if the opposition team are coming into it with a particularly grim record themselves, a winless run for example, else a spell of games without even scoring a goal, then that poor sequence will undoubtedly come to an end when they play Norwich...*" One example of this bizarre law of football was the visit of Bradford City to Carrow Road on January 10th 2004. Bradford came to the game one place off the bottom of the Championship, had only won three of their last 20 fixtures and had only scored eight goals in their away league fixtures all season. Norwich, in contrast, were top of the table and had just won four games on the bounce scoring 11 goals and conceding only two in their previous eight outings. So what happened? Well, Norwich lost, of course, 1-0, with Alun Armstrong, on loan to Bradford from Ipswich Town (it could only be him) scoring the decisive goal.

CHATHAM SUNK

NON-league Chatham came to Norwich twice in FA Cup ties in the 1920s, but were sent packing on each occasion, Norwich winning 5-0 in their second-round tie in the 1926/27 season, and 6-1 in the first round two seasons later. In that 1927 tournament, Norwich went one better in the second round, beating Newport County 6-0, Percy 'give it to' Varco scoring four of the goals.

FRIENDS REUNITED

MEL Machin and Dave Stringer were teammates in the Norwich side that lost 1-0 to Aston Villa in the 1975 League Cup Final. Fourteen years later, the same tournament brought the pair together again, this time as opposing managers as Norwich, with Stringer at the helm, played Machin's Manchester City in a third-round tie at Maine Road. On this occasion, Machin was the happier of the two as his side won 3-1, Robert Fleck, who was nine on the day of that 1975 clash, scoring a late consolation for the Canaries.

GIVEN HARLEY A CHANCE

CENTRE forward Alex Harley joined Norwich from Connah's Quay in 1930, with a prolific and consistent goalscoring record behind him. Three years prior to joining Norwich, he had scored 43 goals in one season for Caernavon and after a brief spell with New Brighton was carrying on in much the same vein for Connah's Quay. He made his Norwich debut in a 2-2 home draw against Coventry City on September 20th, failing to score, but with most Norwich fans expecting him to be given chances to establish himself in the side. Not so. That first match for the club was also his last and two months after signing him, Norwich cancelled his registration.

GO WEST, YOUNG MAN

STRIKER Roger Gibbins became one of a growing number of English-based footballers who tried their luck in the United States in the 1970s, leaving Norwich to join the New England Teamen in March 1978. Gibbins, another ex-Tottenham player to have flourished at Carrow Road, joined Norwich from Oxford United on a free transfer in June 1976, making his debut in the 3-1 Carrow Road defeat to Arsenal on August 25th. He scored his first goal on October 16th, a consolation, as Norwich lost at home to Leeds United, 2-1. Gibbins ended the season with five goals from 20 league appearances. His North American Soccer League (NASL) records for the two summers he spent with the Teamen were; 49 games played, eight goals scored. He was also credited with eight 'assists'. Amongst Gibbins' teammates during the time with the Teamen were Canary goalkeeping legend Kevin Keelan and former Leicester City striker Keith Weller.

NOT *MATCH OF THE DAY*

WITH Norwich comfortably sitting in second place in Division Two, with only one defeat in their first 15 league games the BBC, probably reluctantly, chose to come to Carrow Road to check out their promotion challenge; the Carrow Road clash with Bristol Rovers being selected for *Match of the Day* coverage on November 9th 1974. Norwich were unable to raise their game for either the TV cameras, the 21,172 present, or the watching nation slipping to a 1-0 defeat, their first Carrow Road loss in the league that promotion season.

ON THE BALL!

'ON The Ball' is the name of the much respected Norwich City programme that is devised, written, and printed in time for every home league and cup match. It regularly contains features about the club and players, as well as interviews that are not available in any other printed format, so it is a 'must have' item for all Norwich supporters wanting to keep right up-to-date with events going on at Carrow Road, as well as the club's training complex at Colney. The programme has a distinguished history, having won the Football Programme Directory 'Programme of the Year' award in the Championship for both the 2003/04 and 2006/07 seasons, as well as winning the then First Division Programme of the Year award in 1980/81. As well as being available in and around the ground on match days, it is also on sale in the club's stores at Carrow Road and in the Castle Mall shopping complex, in central Norwich. To keep up with the demand of Canary fans 'in exile' all over the world, it is also available on a subscription basis through the club's online shop. The average print run is around 8,000 per match. Numerous match programmes that feature Norwich City are of interest to collectors; one example is the 1959 FA Cup semi-final match between Norwich and Luton Town, which sells for around £25-£30 (2010). In sharp contrast to that, a programme for the Canaries' 1989 semi-final clash with Everton can be bought for around £2. Two of the most valuable Norwich programmes relate to the 1962 League Cup Final with Rochdale. The programmes produced for each leg remain rare with the away programme from the first leg often fetching over £1,000 at auctions.

Saturday, April 9, 2005   KO 5.15pm   vs Manchester United

On The Ball

Official Matchday Programme

£3.00

www.canaries.co.uk

LOTUS CARS

PROTON CARS

MEN IN TIGHTS

NORWICH'S FA Cup third-round tie against then lower division Leicester City on January 6th 1979 would not have drawn the BBC *Match of the Day* cameras had not many of the day's other games been cancelled due to the icy weather at the time, but in turning up at Filbert Street they captured one of the more forgettable days of John Bond's Norwich reign. Leicester striker Keith Weller dressed for the occasion, donning black tights to combat the freezing conditions and despite whatever stick he might have got from the crowd or Norwich players for doing so, he dominated proceedings, Leicester easily winning, 3-0.

BEATING BURNLEY

NORWICH first played Burnley at their Turf Moor ground on April 27th 1935, losing 1-0. It was to be nearly 70 years before the Canaries would make that away trip and return with a league win, that first victory coming in April 2004 with Norwich top of the First Division, emphasising their promotion credentials with a convincing 5-3 victory.

LE TISSIER'S FIRST

MATT Le Tissier made his league debut for Southampton in their 4-3 defeat at Norwich on August 30th 1986. Kevin Drinkell, Dale Gordon, David Williams and Steve Bruce the Norwich scorers, the game marking the official opening of the new Main Stand, following the destruction of the old stand by fire nearly two years earlier.

IWAN'S FINALE

IN his 20-year career, Canaries striker Iwan Roberts had never scored on the final day of a league campaign. That is until his last-ever game for Norwich City. Roberts made his farewell as Norwich, already Division One champions, beat Crewe Alexandra 3-1 on the last day of the 2003/04 season with the Welshman scoring twice. Roberts later spoke of his first goal, a left-foot half-volley, saying "I don't think I've scored a better one in a Norwich City shirt, to be honest!" The Crewe goal on the day was scored by the man destined to replace Roberts: Dean Ashton netting in the second half.

THE END OF SHIRTS 1-11

THE system of allocating each player in a club's squad a specific number which he retained throughout that season was introduced into the Premiership for the start of the 1993/94 season. The final matches of the 1992/93 campaign were therefore the last opportunity for fans to see their teams line up with the 'traditional' numbering sequence of one through to eleven on the back of their shirts. The Canaries played their last game under the 'old' numbering system on May 8th, against Middlesbrough at Ayresome Park. Norwich lined up as follows: 1. Gunn; 2.Culverhouse; 3. Bowen; 4. Newman; 5. Polston; 6. Johnson; 7. Crook; 8. Sutton; 9. Ekoku; 10. Fox and 11. Phillips. The match ended 3-3 (the point ensuring Norwich finished third), Efan Ekoku (2) and Andy Johnson scoring for the Canaries.

ALL NEW SQUAD NUMBERS

PLAYERS, management and fans therefore had to get used to each player having his own, unique squad number for the 1993/94 season (see above), rather than the number signifying his position (e.g) number five = centre half, number nine = centre forward etc. For their first match of that Premiership season, a televised game at home to Manchester United, the Canaries lined up as follows: 1. Gunn; 5. Culverhouse; 2. Bowen; 17. Butterworth; 10. Polston; 11. Goss; 4. Crook; 3. Newman; 12. Robins; 14. Fox and 22. Sutton. The Canaries substitute that day, Efan Ekoku, wore the number 7 shirt, taking the place of Mark Robins who, ironically, had the squad number of 12, long synonymous with the position of substitute – whether Robins had asked for that number or not, is unknown! Roy Keane, wearing the number 16 shirt, made his Manchester United debut in that match.

DUTCH UPSET

FRANS Thijssen, one half of Ipswich Town's famous Dutch midfield pairing (alongside Arnold Muhren) scored his first-ever goal for the Blues in their 1-0 win over Norwich on April 14th 1979, the only goal of a tight game at Carrow Road. During the match, Canaries centre-half David Jones was booked. Nothing unusual about that, you may think, except that Jones wasn't even playing, his off-pitch comments made about the referee were overheard, thus earning him that unfortunate yellow card.

CREWE CUT CANARIES

NORWICH'S Division One match at Crewe Alexandra on January 9th 1999 seemed to be going to form, first-half strikes from Chris Llewellyn and Lee Marshall had given the Canaries a comfortable lead and with less than ten minutes to go, victory seemed assured. Bottom-of-the-table Crewe had other ideas, and put some late pressure on. Kevin Street pulled the score back to 3-1; future Norwich signing Mark Rivers made it 2-2 in the 87th minute, and, just when it looked as if Norwich were going to get away with a draw, Street scored again in injury time, slotting home the winner after Canary goalkeeper Michael Watt parried Shaun Smith's free kick into his path. It turned out to be the unfortunate Watt's final game for Norwich.

DEFENCES BREACHED!

THE Canaries made a flying start to the 2002/03 season, winning four and drawing two of their first six league games and only conceding two goals in the process; testament indeed to the stable back four of Nedergaard, Kenton, Fleming and Drury. The Carrow Road clash against Sheffield United on September 7th saw that defence breached as many times in the opening five minutes as it had previously been all season, goals by Michaels Brown and Tonge doing the damage. Carl Asaba netted a penalty on the half hour and the Blades never looked back, late goals by Malky Mackay and Paul McVeigh giving the score a little respectability. Nigel Worthington brought in Malky Mackay in place of Fleming for the next match, a 1-1 draw at Ipswich Town. Mackay scored the Norwich goal. The Canaries then scored twice in the opening five minutes themselves, in a 2-0 home win over Reading on September 18th, Phil Mulryne and Paul McVeigh doing the honours. The defeated Reading team on that day featured two players who would later join the Canaries; Andy Hughes, and for a second spell Jamie Cureton.

DAREL'S DEBUT

MIDFIELDER Darel Russell made his Canaries debut in the 1-0 win at Reading on May 3rd 1998 as a second-half substitute for loan striker Neale Fenn. He scored his first goal for Norwich in the 1-1 draw with Huddersfield Town on March 24th 1999.

CULT HERO!

IN 2005, the BBC's *Football Focus* programme launched a nationwide vote to find out which players fans thought was their club's all-time 'cult hero'. Goalkeeper Bryan Gunn narrowly won the Norwich fans vote with 37% of those cast just pipping Iwan Roberts, who got 36%. Robert Fleck came in third place, with 27% of the votes.

FRANCIS FOILED

TREVOR Francis, who would ultimately become the first £1 million player in British football, lined up for his first club Birmingham City, in their Division One game against Norwich on March 20th 1974. He had a mixed game winning a penalty for Birmingham which he took – and missed – in the second half. Norwich won 2-1, with goals from Boyer and Suggett.

TOP MAN

MALCOLM Allen scored more FA Cup goals for Norwich than any other player in the 1980s, even though all seven of his goals came in the one campaign! Norwich's run to the semi-finals in the 1988/89 season saw him score four against Sutton United, one against Sheffield United and two in the quarter-final replay victory over West Ham United. During the 1990s, 16 different players scored FA Cup goals for the Canaries, with Robert Fleck leading the way with seven goals.

BY GEORGE!

GEORGE Travers was the leading scorer for Norwich in season 1920/21, with 14 strikes from his 29 league games – a great achievement when you consider he only joined the club in late October of that season, the club's first as a fully-fledged league club. His first goal came in the 1-0 win over Reading on November 6th 1920, the club's first win of the season, and as a league club.

MORE 100s

CHRIS Sutton scored Norwich's 100th Premiership goal. His – and the team's – second in a 3-3 draw at West Ham United on January 24th 1994.

ROY OF THE CANARIES

ROY Hollis scored 16 goals from just 33 league appearances for Norwich in the 1950/51 season including a remarkable sequence of seven goals in just four games, the highlight of that run being a first-half hat-trick in the home match against Southend United on November 18th. He also scored a hat-trick on his City debut, a 5-2 Carrow Road win over Queens Park Rangers on April 21st 1948, those three goals coming in just 20 minutes. Hollis didn't just score hat-tricks. When Norwich demolished Walsall 8-0 on January 29th 1951, he scored five, ending that season with 20 goals from 27 league matches. And, true to form, when he played his final City match on March 8th 1952, he scored one of the goals as the Canaries won at Northampton, 2-1. Ironically, his last hat-trick in a game featuring the Canaries was for Southend United; Hollis and his new team thoroughly spoiling the festivities on Christmas Day 1954 with a 4-1 win; his three goals on that day making him the first player to score three goals for, <u>and</u> against, Norwich at Carrow Road.

DANNY BOY

DEFENDER Danny Mills made 73 appearances for Norwich, initially coming to first team prominence when he was named, at just 17, as one of the substitutes for Norwich's Premiership game at Everton on November 5th 1994. That game ended 0-0 (Everton, and former Norwich boss Mike Walker was sacked just two days later) and turned out to be the closest Mills got to first-team action that season. He made his full debut on the opening day of the following campaign as Norwich were back in Division One and hoping to get off to a winning start under their new manager Martin O'Neill in the game at Luton Town. Mills was prominent enough giving away the penalty that gave Luton their equaliser. Luckily for him, Norwich won the game 3-1. That first full season at Carrow Road saw Mills make 17 league and cup appearances, his first goal coming in a 4-0 League Cup win over Torquay United. Mills joined Charlton Athletic in 1998 before moving onto Leeds United, playing in every minute of England's five matches at the 2002 World Cup finals – not a bad achievement for a Norwich-born lad and product of the Norwich City School of Excellence!

GLENN'S GOAL

FUTURE Norwich manager Glenn Roeder scored the only goal of the game as Queens Park Rangers won 1-0 at Carrow Road on February 27th 1982. Two future Norwich bosses were in the Canaries side that day too; Martin O'Neill and John Deehan.

BIG DEFEAT, BIG WIN

THE surest way to get over any big defeat in football is to 'put it right' in the following game, and the Canaries duly did that following a shock 4-0 reverse at Swansea City in their Division One game on September 4th 1982. No doubt a few well chosen words from Ken Brown helped do the trick as, just four days later, Birmingham City came to Carrow Road and were soundly beaten 5-1. The Canaries duly got some sort of revenge in the return game against Swansea on January 3rd 1983, winning 1-0 via a Mike Channon strike. The veteran Channon made 20 league appearances for the Canaries that season, scoring three goals.

FIRST VERSUS SECOND

WHEN Norwich hosted Arsenal in a Division One fixture on December 10th 1988, it was a game that the country had been waiting for, first versus second in the table, and a severe test for both sides. The game was a big anti-climax. Arsenal came closest to scoring, and, indeed did when Brian Marwood slotted home a penalty. He was ordered to retake it and promptly missed. Norwich duly picked themselves up after this disappointing result by travelling to Liverpool for their next league game, the 1-0 win, courtesy of an Andy Townsend strike, consolidating the Canaries' place on top of Division One. As for Arsenal? They ended that season as Division One champions, beating Liverpool into second place on goal difference. Norwich, much to everyone's surprise, maintained their lofty position in the league and ended up finishing fourth in what was perhaps the club's greatest-ever season coming, as it did, with an appearance in an FA Cup semi-final. The club were doing so well at one stage that the bookies of the nation were taking bets on the possibility of Norwich City doing the double! Dave Stringer had, unquestionably, sowed the seed that was to be Mike Walker's to ultimately reap…

LOAN AGAIN

THE very first player that Norwich brought to the club on loan was Bobby Bell, who joined from Crystal Palace for a month in February 1972. Bell made three appearances in that time.

ASHMAN (PEN)

AS well as holding the record for the most appearances by an outfield player for Norwich, Ron Ashman was a penalty king for the team, scoring a total of 17 from the spot from May 1951 to April 1954.

KEN CAN

NORWICH'S first game in Division Two was against Brentford, where Ken Burditt took the honours for scoring the club's first goal at that level, netting the consolation in a 2-1 away defeat at Brentford.

GUNN'S CLEAN SHEETS

WHEN the Canaries drew 0-0 at Liverpool on September 16th 1989, Bryan Gunn became the first goalkeeper since Gordon Banks to keep three successive clean sheets at Anfield.

IN SHORT

A MAJOR decision made at the club AGM in 1969 was to change the colour of the team's shorts from green to black. The reasoning given was that black shorts stayed smarter, for longer, than green ones!

CARROW ROAD'S FIRST

THE first match played at Carrow Road saw Norwich defeat West Ham United 4-3, in front of 29,779 people on August 31st 1935. Doug Lochhead was Norwich captain.